A Guide's Tale

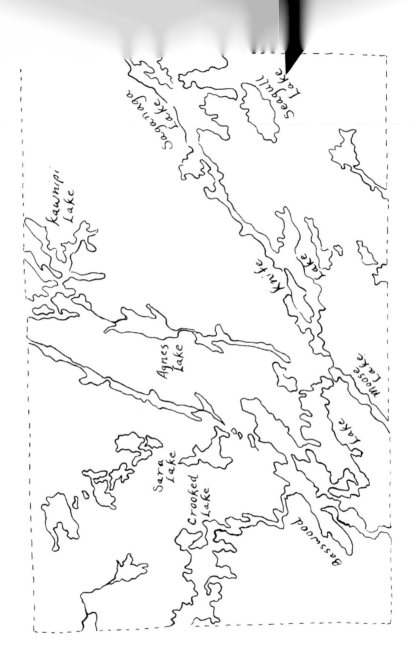

A Guide's Tale

Gerald R. Patterson

VANTAGE PRESS
New York

FIRST EDITION

Copyright © 2009 by Gerald R. Patterson

Published by Vantage Press, Inc.
419 Park Ave. South, New York, NY 10016

Manufactured in the United States of America
ISBN: 978-0-533-16101-0

Library of Congress Catalog Card No: 2008906547

0 9 8 7 6 5 4 3 2 1

To my mother and all others who hug trees

Contents

1. Fall Trout: First Glimpse   1
2. The Family at Robinson Lake   26
3. The Novice   51
4. The Apprentice   59
5. War   108
6. Return to Quetico   140

A Guide's Tale

1

Fall Trout: First Glimpse

The country lay at the edge of things. It was that stubborn spot on maps of northern Minnesota where ruled lines stop and map boundaries follow the organic lines dictated by rivers and the edges of great lakes. Below the country laid the land where the glaciers died. My family lived in a collection of cabins sprinkled around three small lakes interconnected by several creeks and a stream. Of the thirty-one people who lived there, twenty-eight were relatives.

If you started in a canoe from the family lake basin, you could travel north all the way to Hudson's Bay. For some members of the family, that open space on the map pulled like a magnet. It meant there were no boundaries there. The wilderness to the north was an extension of our lake basin. Each person who lived in the lake basin set his own boundaries. The result was a family with more than its share of restless spirits, each finding their own unique path. When Uncle Hank was a boy, he took a trip with old Martin, the fur trapper living down at the end of Robinson Lake. They canoed across the west end of the lake, portaged north into Wolf Lake, and then just kept going till they hit the Indian village on Lac La Croix eighty miles away. They got all the way to the chain of lakes that formed the old voyageur highway coming down from Lake Athabasca.

It was hard country scraped by glaciers right down to greenstone, some of earth's oldest crust. The high ridges around

Robinson Lake ran more or less north and south on either side of the basin. The harsh lines of these rock spines were gentled by a covering of birch, poplar and some maple. The fall colors up on the high ridges gave the feeling that the country was still very young. Here and there were small pockets of dark green pine, left over from the invasion by logging companies at the turn of the century. It was the logging that brought in the flood of Norwegian immigrants, including Grandpa Nicholson. Much of the country between the ridges was given over to small pothole lakes and endless swamps with their tiny boreal spruce. You could pretty much count on snow for eight or nine months of the year. That, plus the starvation-thin coating of topsoil, made it a purgatory for farmers.

It was an immense, lonely place, so it was easy to understand why families like ours clustered in little pockets along the highways and the railroad tracks. Driving at night, there would be light in a window, then two or three more followed again by deep blackness. There would usually only be that one lamp lit per window, as there was no electricity in those days.

All of the men had full-time jobs in the iron mines, railroads, or logging camps, but during the Depression, there was never enough money, and never any certainty that a job would still be there in a month. In the spring, summer, and fall, most of the men took on extra jobs to bring in money guiding on the big lakes, trapping, or hiring out as carpenters. It was in this spirit that the family pooled their talents and constructed two tiny resorts on the largest of the three lakes in the basin. All of the uncles in the family combined forces to put up the cabins. This labor of desperation was designed to siphon off a tiny trickle of the immense wealth that flowed right by our doorstep. In the spring, as soon as the snow melted, the lines of cars would begin moving up from the cities to the south. You could hear the whine from the tires in the evening as they hit the long stretch just before Robinson Lake.

The tide of wealth never came in; there was just no compelling reason for the tourists to stop and leave money in what was essentially a collection of homemade cabins, woodsheds, and icehouses. We considered building some fences to make a zoo for wild animals, but most of the animals that we had around there looked pretty tacky in the summertime. Even the bears walked around with their fur looking like a toupee that just didn't fit. We considered getting old Purvis to come out of his swamp, sitting him under a tree wearing his red kerchief around the neck and his Spanish American war campaign hat, and just letting him talk. We figured that if we could just get people to stop, old Purvis would never let them leave. That man loved an audience, but only when he felt like talking. His basic flaw was his unpredictability as a host. The family used to pack supplies six miles into the big spruce swamp where he had his cabin. If he were feeling out of sorts, he would just stand up on the ridge behind his cabin and whang rifle shots over their heads. That was a signal that he wasn't really up to having company. You just never knew till you arrived. This was, unfortunately not a dependable way to make a fortune.

The new cabins fed into my mother's already rich fantasy life. It was a feverish spring, and one in which she presided over countless coffee sessions attended by family members. They planned the royal brick road to wealth, central heating, and maybe even a flush toilet. There was some concern that three cabins might not be sufficient to meet the demand. It gradually emerged that the key to the whole enterprise was services. We would rent them boats, sell them minnows for fishing, and maybe hire out as fish guides to show them where Robinson Lake's trophy Northern pike were to be found.

That spring, before the crows got back, my dad and almost all of the uncles spent every spare minute and their weekends putting up three cabins. As you drove along the lakeshore, you could see our family cabin with its porch. The three log-sided cabins were set up on the small knoll at the end of the point. Two fancy outhouses set behind the ice house could not be seen from the road.

It turned out that this was a pretty hard way to make money, particularly given the way my mother had worked out the details. The problem lay in her basic confusion between making money and making friends. You might say that in her case, avarice was overwhelmed by love. What made her such a marvelous mother and friend led to automatic failure when she served as business administrator. When a carload of tourists would drive in from the road, she would be out the door in her white apron, a tiny figure with blonde hair and a big smile. She would show them all of the wonders of her new cabins and her lake (she always called it this, as she had been born close by): "You turn on the gas stove this way . . . Yes, and my sons will fetch the water for you from the spring up the hill." As she rushed along, she would be overcome by her own enthusiasm to the point where the boats that were supposed to be rented were thrown into the deal for free. If the visitors looked a little down on their luck, the minnows for sale became minnows for free. The big money for showing them where the Northern pike could be found turned into, "Jerry here will take you out fishing after supper. He knows every fish in the lake by name." There was never any mention of any money. All the guests were treated as if they were part of the Robinson Lake family. My mother was so enthusiastic about sharing her cabins, her lake, and her life that many of them would end up staying just because of her. If they stayed for a day or two, she would bring them a blueberry pie, or whatever else was in season. I always felt like she was adopting these people, not renting to them.

Some of the tourists didn't look like they would be a great joy to take fishing, either. I would always try to get out of it. At that point, all of her five-foot-two frame would tower over me: "Well, we told them that we would take them fishing. That means that we will." I would stand there thinking of all those "we's," and not know quite how to begin. "That is what a man is," she'd say. "If he says he will do something, then he has got to do it." She wasn't angry—just surprised that I was even thinking of not following up on

4

her promise. There was no argument; she just walked into the house to start on the next part of her money-from-tourists project.

As soon as the tourists left, my mother and one of the aunts would take all the sheets off the beds, haul water from the lake, and wash them. It would be midday before the washing, the ironing, and the sweeping and mopping were done. They would then sit in exhausted silence waiting for the next big spenders to drive up.

My mother kept the tourist money in a bowl in the cupboard. Each fall, she would proudly take the bowl down and count up the summer's profits. She eventually paid off the cost of the cabins and the boats. She kept it going long after the rest of us understood that this was not the royal road to wealth. Some of the visitors we had adopted her in turn. Each Christmas, she would receive cards from all over the Midwest. Many of them returned each summer and literally became part of the family. I'm pretty sure that at some point she no longer charged them for the cabins, but none of us ever asked her. She had a special magic about her that made you want to be a part of how she saw things.

When the sumac and maple leaves began to show handfuls of red here and there, and the birches showcased a hint of yellow, it was time to begin three of the Robinson Lake family rituals. All the men and boys would collect in one place and cut down enough birch trees to supply each family through the winter. The women would come to each house in turn with enough stew and home-made bread to fuel the day's sawing and piling. A family's wealth was defined by how tight and well-made this house was and by the size of the woodpile behind it.

Ice was a family affair that came later in the fall. In Minnesota lake country the temperature would drop below zero for weeks. Sometimes this happened before the snow came and would turn the whole lake into a giant skating rink. It was wondrous, gliding under the black night with the stars in close, skating with your face down close to the ice, moving your arms back and forth to balance the long strides, the ice grumbling and thundering under

5

your feet, and the cold a mask just under your eyes and across your cheeks. Everything was pinpointed in the perfect moment, when you were a part of all of it.

The snows usually arrived around freeze-up time. Then it became the task of a platoon of younger boys to keep the snow shoveled off the ice, so that it would freeze as deeply as possible. When it was about three or four feet thick, one of the uncles would show up with a six foot metal bar with a chisel welded to the end. A black figure standing out there on the ice, feet spread wide apart, you could hear the sound of his chisel thunking, then echoing across the lake. The water, almost black, oozed into the bottom of the basin carved into the ice. If the ice was thick enough, all the men in the village would come to our cabin with ice saws, chisels, ropes, and pulleys. Ice cutting went on all day long. Some of the uncles would set tongs to the ice floating in black water and haul the chunks off to the icehouses. There were two or three ice saws going all the time, cutting straight lines into the ice. It was far enough below zero, that the men would just keep streaming in and out of the house. Smells of baking bread and meat wafted from the oven; the house was jammed with aunts, kids, and uncles and the tables covered by coffee thermoses, cakes, and cookies. I noticed that the men often veered off to our woodshed to emerge a few minutes later with satisfied smiles. My cousins and I were not invited to join.

Before the ice cutting and the wood cutting there was the matter of putting in the fall meat and fall lake trout. Making fall trout meant making a lightning dash up to the border lakes and returning with several hundred pounds of lake trout caught on hand lines. The women would can the fish and it would last all winter. On very special days the jar would come out and you could smell the fish cakes cooking on the wood stove. In the winter months, the men would sit around telling stories about the hunting and the fishing. Many of the stories included such strange names such as Lac

6

Le Croix; Knife Lake; or the chain of lakes This Man, That Man, and The Other Man.

It was never labeled and seldom talked about, but each of my cousins and I were involved in a carefully crafted apprenticeship. My uncles and my father were the teachers. The process was designed to convert promising raw material into a presence that would be useful on a lake, a trap line, or a canoe trip. My Uncle Hugo had carefully tutored me for two summers now on how to paddle the canoe in a straight line while someone was fishing in the bow. In that Hugo was usually the someone in the bow, fishing for walleyes while I learned to paddle, the system was well designed for enlightened self interest, both for young boys and aging uncles. Hugo had married into the family. He had no children of his own. A quiet person, he nevertheless loved to have kids around. The delicate bones in his face, and the skin folded along the inside corner of his eye gave him a gentle, almost exotic look. There was always an air of sadness about him. Perhaps as a young boy I just confused quietness with sadness.

But Hugo was plagued by bad luck. For example, a month before deer season he bought a new pump action 30–06 that would allow him to get a lot of lead in the air in a very short time. He was outlawing before the deer season opened. He found his deer, but couldn't resist the temptation to fire a whole burst. Everyone knows that before the season you take your deer with a single round so the game warden could not locate you. The warden just happened to be driving by when Hugo lost control. He not only lost the new rifle, but had to hear about the incident at almost every family gathering where drinks were exchanged, year after year.

I was twelve years old before Hugo pronounced me ready. In my newly elevated status, I could now go along as a paddler on the fall trips for lake trout. In fact, I was told I was going to be a paddler for my grandfather. My father couldn't go on the trip, but gave a huge grin when he heard that I was going. He walked over to the closet and took out the thick wool shirt Mom had given him

7

last Christmas, "Here kid—better take this. It's gonna be cold up there." Nothing more was said. Mother had me carry the lake water to a tub sitting on the stove. When the water was hot, I carried it outside to the Maytag washing machine sitting behind the cabin. I would start the trip with clean clothes. She baked bread that night and sent two loaves along in my pack.

We left Robinson Lake in trucks before dawn. The plan was to be up on the Canadian border in time for fishing by mid-afternoon. The Echo Trail road was basically a long dirt track winding north into small hills, smaller lakes, and thickening fingers of swamps. The river itself was not very impressive. It held almost no current. Its thick brown water seemed to hold back the grass and weeds crowding the shoreline along the giant loops it made through the swamp. As we moved north there were more frequent rock outcroppings touched by glaciers; clean, freshly scoured rock standing in the midst of dark forest.

By the time the light first cut the mist on the Nina Moose River, we were all in canoes and moving down river. As the mist burned off, we had already arrived at the short portage into Nina Moose Lake. My Uncle Hank's canoe was in front. It had a side bracket behind the stern seat with a three-horsepower engine hanging down in the water. At the portage, Hank switched off the engine and flipped the tow rope over his shoulder. He stood up with his paddle in his hands and slowly worked the canoe into shore. It had never been discussed, nor was it written down anywhere, but it was crystal clear to everyone that Uncle Hank was the family leader. He and his brother Buster planned the wood cutting, the fall trout trips, the deer hunting, and much of the beaver trapping for the family. Hank was several inches short of six feet, but he had the habit of looking you straight in the eye no matter how tall you grew. His pale blue eyes and the slight smile that went with them left no doubt that the two of you were really the same size; in fact, you were probably even a little shorter than he was. Hank was a competitor—you knew that by his handshake and most everything else he did. He set standards for himself that the rest of us simply could not meet. Later, when he was in his eighties, he was still doing chin-ups by hanging from the trim over the doorway.

Of the eight children born to Grandma at Robinson Lake, one died and one left to live in a city in the West; but the other six remained living in the lake basin. As each married, the family would find or build a home for them, so they could stay. The friends, relatives, and tourists who came to visit envied the extraordinary freedom the lake basin provided especially if you were male and even doubly so if you were a boy, but they could not see the invisible halters and hobbles that kept the family there. It was more comfortable to stay there, protected by the family, than to take the risk of leaving. Each member was free to develop within a narrow set of boundaries defining what was acceptable, but there was little hope of encountering a model that was much different from what had come before. You could not be different. What we were doing on the canoe trip was much as the previous generation had done it. Individually, each of us carried a sense of pride in the fact that we belonged to this particular family.

Grandpa sat in the bow of our canoe. He coiled the towrope and slid it behind him into the top of a Duluth pack. Hank's younger brother, Buster paddled us toward the shore. Bus was taller and maybe twenty pounds heavier than Hank. He smiled a lot; always beaming a huge grin on a big square face. Buster had smile marks deep on his face before he was thirty.

Each canoe was eighteen feet long, and each contained two men and a boy. Like me, this was my cousin Sonny's first trip. We had moved smoothly through the country all morning. At each portage, we performed the same quiet ritual. The man in the bow—my grandfather, in our canoe, would stand up and in the same motion step over the side, into the water. Usually, this came up over his boot tops. He would then simply stand there in the September water holding the canoe. A glance in my direction meant I was to do the same. Holding on to the gunwale, I would slip and splash my way over to him. Grandpa was taller than the rest of us, but not built as heavily as my uncles. His washed-out blue denim shirt was crossed in the back with thick suspenders that held up his heavy wool staged pants. He returned and lifted a Duluth pack out of the canoe. Buster stood, leaned as far forward as he could, and placed both hands on the gunwale. Then he brought his feet up on the gunwales and crab-walked his way over the top of the mountain of packs in front of him. He'd always have a big grin as he stepped into the water in front of me, "Don't want to break them eggs," he'd say. He would pick up the second pack behind the thwart and swing it around his side and behind him. All the packs and gear from our canoe were stacked in one place so it could not get mixed up with the gear from Hank's canoe, or with anyone else's on the portage.

Our canoe weighed eighty-five pounds when absolutely dry. If it had rained for three or four days, it weighed well over a hundred. With its spruce ribs curving up to the gunwales and the thin cedar strips bending into the bow, it seemed like there were no straight lines in it, anywhere. Each spring, its canvas exterior was sanded and given a new coat of green paint. It was always handled gently. If you worked in the iron mines, a canoe would cost a month's salary. Each of these ancient beauties had been in the family for a long time. Their patched bottoms spoke of reefs encountered unexpectedly in mid-lake, and of wind-lashed shorelines where survival demands outweighed the love for the canoe. Each canoe carried its own can of repair pitch in a sack tied up under the bow. You could tell where a canoe was on the portage by the sound of the pitch can tapping against the bow.

The first morning of the ritual, Grandpa slipped the big Duluth pack up on his thighs and worked one arm through one strap. He gave a twist as he came around and thrust his left arm into the remaining strap. "Jeddy, is this one for you?" he asked in a soft voice, with a hint of a smile, as he lifted the lightweight kettle pack out of our canoe. I sat it on the ground to watch him make his next move. He waded out to the canoe, lifted out the last pack, and brought it to shore. Holding it between his legs by its ears, he swung it gently, and thrust his knees against it as it came forward. "Ja, ja, a lit snoose, and there she go." With that he swung it in an arc over his head to settle on top of the pack on his back. He turned up the bank, looked at me and gave an emphatic nod, "Yah, like so, Jeddy. Yah?" I put my light personal pack on my back and then walked over to the kettle pack with its axe handle sticking out on one side. I picked it up by its ears and tried to swing it, but it bumped against my knees and dropped back to the ground. No one offered to help; they didn't even appear to notice. I spread my twelve-year-old legs as wide apart as they would go and swung it again. It went high up in the air and came down against my back with a crash of kettles and frying pans. The force of it spun me around, and I staggered off in tiny jerking steps trying to catch up to the momentum of the pack. Buster had been standing in the water to waiting to see the outcome, "Pa, we gotta feed that kid more beans or he'll never paddle you for lake trout." He laughed and reached down to pick up the canoe by its center thwart and slide it up on his thighs. His right arm went deep around the bottom, cradling it like an infant. When it was balanced, he rocked once, then twice, and pivoted to his left as he straightened up. The canoe went up in the air over his head, and came down squarely on his shoulders. He reached over and took the two paddles that Grandpa handed him and shot them smartly up under the seat so the blades went deep into the bow. He was already moving as the paddles rattled into place; he passed me at the first bend in the trail.

Natives, the people that live in and around Ely, pride themselves on their ability to move across portages quickly. When they organize a canoe race, portaging is usually a part of it. Both the packer and the canoe carrier move across the rocky trail in a mincing shuffle stop that is really more of a half run. These are the same movements made by the voyageurs who worked this country two

11

hundred years earlier. If you ask Ely natives about this, they will probably say that if you move fast there is less time for the pain to build, or for the mosquitoes to find you. But the running shuffle on portages is really a little statement that says you are good enough to be in that place. It's a prideful thing to move smoothly with a hundred pounds on your back, performing a small dance from one rock to the next with no break in stride.

The portage ritual is carefully orchestrated to minimize the picking up and setting down of heavy packs. For example, the canoe carrier makes it a point to get across first. He wades out and slides the canoe across his thighs into the water. He removes the balance paddles from under the bow seat and then drops his light personal pack in front of the stern seat. By this time, the double packer arrives and drops one of his heavy food packs in front of the stern thwart and the other ahead of the yoke. This leaves a small pocket for the third person, who places one pack in the front section and uses the other as a seat. There are no wasted motions here. The packs are not placed on the ground and then lifted into the canoe. The least effort is to drop it from your back directly into the canoe. It is all done without words, as if previously arranged by a choreographer.

Traveling by canoe is natural. My father and most of my uncles were trappers, and if you trap, you travel by canoe. When canoe racing became a fad in Minnesota, it was natural for my family to compete. They designed and built their own racing canoes. Some of the family still compete and are in the upper echelon of professional canoe racers. For a while, during the spring and summer, the family traveled from one race to another and sponsored more than a dozen racers. They won some and lost many, but never really made enough to pay for their travel and partying expenses.

There was one memorable race that began with all the canoes carefully lined up next to each other. On the film, you can see two chunky racers in the canoe next to my brother Mike and cousin

Ray. The two guys were so carried away with the excitement of the moment that when the starting gun went off, they began literally shoveling water into Mike's canoe. He yelled at them but they didn't seem to hear him. The high point of the film is Mike standing up and hurtling his six-foot frame into their racing shell. You can see Mike trying to land a punch as the canoe turns over.

Very early, each of us developed a sense of pride in being a member of the family. Belonging to my family made you an elitist. During the fall hunt, I had once seen Uncle Hank shoot three running deer. How many men could do a thing like that? All of the skills we needed to survive were right there in the family. My father understood electricity and eventually wired the houses that the family built for themselves. Uncle Frank knew about guns and how to fix them. Bus could fix any kind of machine. All of the family owned their own houses; they built them one by one as they were needed. We stayed mainly out of trouble aside from a series of barroom brawls with the notorious Yonklavich family. There were some who claimed that Uncle Hank might have started the last one. In the spirit of good fun, he had gone into the bar and cut off everybody's ties with his belt knife, one by one. As he saw it, the whole thing was a genteel way of getting people to loosen up and have fun. The Yonklavich brothers used his action as an excuse to start trouble. The discussion that followed in the alley behind the bar somehow produced a broken nose for my father. He was taking his coat off as he came through the door; it is said that he didn't contribute much to the meeting that followed. Several uncles and cousins spent that evening in jail. Only a boy at the time, it was difficult for me to get the details straight, but I do remember Grandma dressed in her going-to-town black coat, tiny blue hat with artificial flowers, and huge black purse. Her facial expression was more than grim as she got on the train to go and bail them out of jail.

As we portaged into Lac La Croix, the country had a different feel to it. The glaciers had scoured deep here, hard rock was showing even in the low places between the hills. In the last few portages the trails had followed the ridge tops, with the smell of the pine warming to the noon day sun. From deep inside the kettle pack there was the faint smell of coffee. On the last portage over the top of the ridge, the flat slab of rock was a smooth highway with glaciers' signatures incised everywhere, like ancient runic lines. Far below you could see the flash of big water through the trees.

We traveled with only two canoes which were lashed together by birch poles. One pole was tied off along the front thwart on both canoes and left about ten inches of water between them. The other pole was lashed across the rear thwart in exactly the same way. I had never seen canoeing tied this way before and sat watching as they worked with the ropes. Grandfather sat in the bow of our canoe, tall and lean with his huge handlebar mustache, bending over the tying-off rope behind him. "Ja big water up der. Veree big. It's safer this vay." I liked listening to him talk, each word was softened and slightly blurred so that it almost sounded as if he were actually speaking Norwegian, his first language.

The canoes rode side by side out into the middle of the big water as the wind gradually died off. The water was the color of sky. Far off at the horizon line, you could not tell where the sky ended and the water began. The canoes cut lines in flat water that framed soft white clouds drifting both above and below us. It made you slightly dizzy to look down into the clouds.

Then we moved out into a huge bay of quiet water. My Uncle Hank sat in the back of his canoe running the motor, and his younger brother Buster sat back against the packs in the bow. Uncle Junior sat asleep in the back of our canoe. Hank looked at Grandpa then nodded at the two sleeping figures and cleared his throat with a little cough that meant people were not measuring up. "Long day if you stay up all night partying," he chided. Straight lines started at the bow of Hank's canoe and moved out at a constant angle across the water as we thrummed our way across the bay.

14

Lac La Croix makes a dramatic statement with its range of glaciated rock. The area boasted not just one small cliff here and there that dropped straight down to the water, but dozens. There were twisted slabs of rock piled along beaches and whole ridgelines of great Norway pine ran along the lakeshore to the right of us. We were running parallel to the shore. Bus reached up and tapped me on the shoulder. "Painted cliffs, over there on that island. Indians did it a long time ago." The island to our right looked as if it had been wrenched in half. As we came in closer the cliffs rose above us for a hundred feet. They leaned out a good distance over the water. Pointing with his paddle, he said, "Pretty smart. See, they put their paintings where the rain can't get at them." High up above the waterline on a smooth slab of rock, I could see faint red tracings. They looked like finger drawings a child would make. As art, the drawings were a perfect match for a setting defined by cliffs, big water, and clean rock shelves.

We were thrumming our way through a maze of islands, going south and west. Hank whooped, turned around, and pointed, "Hey, there she is, Coleman Island. Be there soon." There were dozens of rock-shored islands now, all around us, each mysterious and inviting, each different. The two lashed canoes were slicing into a mirror punctuated by rock points and islands. The parallel shock lines coming off the bow and stern stretched far out to each side and gave a sense of motion, but with the huge body of water stretched before us, the shoreline was so distant that you could not be sure you were moving up. Ahead, the infinite mirror surface pulled us into the gap between the mainland and the large landmass Hank had identified as Coleman Island. As we progressed toward it, the last small island that lay ahead of us seemed to be pulled ever so slowly to the right, creating a growing void directly in front of us. It grew moment by moment to expose the largest body of water I had ever seen. It stretched to the north and the west as far as the eye could see. Grandpa turned and took his pipe away to laugh and show me with his hands, "Ja, big water, BIG fish." To the north, the far distant hills showed as a thin blue line almost lost in sky and water. It was like a drummer sounding a faint call. As a boy, it was not yet clear what this call meant. There was just the sense of being pulled to the North—a sense of space and freedom to move. As a young boy, there were no words for this, just a vague mix of joy and restlessness.

We camped in one of the huge bays to the south. The tip of the island just narrowed and shelved into a flat, polished rock that sloped gently down into the water. You could just as easily unload a canoe here as you could take a bath by just walking down the rock shelf until it dropped off into thirty feet of water. We carried the food packs and the kettle pack up to the fireplace to make the kitchen. Grandpa was already building a fire. The well-patched eight-by-ten wall tent was carried over to where Bus and Hank were standing staring at the ground. "Not too bad Bus. Only a few rocks here and they're small ones; just right for young boys." The two birch poles were taken from the canoes and two more cut from back on the hill. Two poles were lashed together at their tips to make an A frame at each end. The sidewalls were folded inside and weighted down with small rocks, and the floor covered with cedar and spruce boughs. The inside of the tent had the thick moist smell of pine.

Each of us made his own bed roll and placed it in the tent while it was still light out. First, a square of canvas was laid on the ground, and then a wool army blanket. A second blanket was laid overlapping half of the first one. The free half of the first then came up and over, and the free half of the second was folded, making a sort of envelope. Both ends were secured with huge bronze safety pins and then rolled up inside the canvas tarp.

By the time we had arrived at Coleman Island it was too late to fish. The sun was already slipping behind the ridge by the time we were wrapping up the dishes down at the lake. There must be a bush law inscribed somewhere stipulating that if is a boy in the camp, he is the one who will end up with the scrubber and the black pots after supper. And so Sonny and I found ourselves hunkered down on our heels at the lakeshore, surrounded by pots and dishes, as the men sat around the fire with their coffee cups and a bottle. "A lit more, Pa. Tux ka da ha." Grandpa filled each of the men's cups and then his own. "Pa, what is the name of the big river that comes in here from the north?" I heard one of my uncles ask. Grandpa was lighting his huge curved pipe. Between clouds of smoke, "Some funny name like Maligne, I think." Hank nodded toward the north end of the lake. Yeah, that sounds right. Old Martin and I came up here all the way from Robinson Lake when I was a kid. We were gone a whole month and ran out of food just as we hit La Croix. There was an Indian village back there and they told us about the big river."

We could hear Buster talking about a network of rivers that ran all the way to Lake Athabasca and on to Hudson's Bay. Only one or two railroads crossed all of that country. No one lived there except some Indians. It was open, free country. I thought about it that night and for many nights afterward. Later, that great core of free, open wilderness became a place to read books about, a focal point for my daydreams in my life as a young man. I read everything about the voyageurs and the North West Territories that I could find. The high country to the north eventually became a part of that subtle fusion of values that emerges and defines who you are, and where you are going.

Grandpa and Hank were out of the tent the next morning before there was light on the water. "Daylight in the swamp. Come on, you fishermen. Coffee is on." For breakfast we had pancakes, thick cuts of bacon from a 10-pound slab, and a boy's mix of coffee, with too much sugar plus heavy squirts from a can of condensed milk. This time, the dishes were left where they fell. The morning wind was already in the trees when we pulled out into the main lake. The favored trout hole lay between two islands not a half-mile from our camp. When we arrived there, Grandpa reached into his pack and took out his fishing tackle: It was 200

17

yards of braided copper wire wrapped tightly around a foot and a half long board that was notched at either end. The line at the end was carefully tied to a swivel snap that held a #4 KB spoon. The spoon, by tradition, is silver on one side and copper on the other. In the water, it looks like a small fish. When placed in the water, the slight bow that defined its length converted cold metal into living movement. Like a kayak or a canoe, the KB spoon is one of those beautiful functional things. Its lines are simple; it needs nothing added to it. Four feet back from the spoon, my Grandpa had carefully tied in a small metal triangle with swivels at each apex. The main copper line and the four feet to the KB were tied to two of them. To the third swivel, he attached about three feet of green fish line. This was tied off to a heavy teardrop sinker.

I slowed down the canoe as Grandpa dropped the spoon and harness gently into the water on the upwind side. The spoon pulsated ever so slowly as it sank into black water, pulled down by the heavy lead pendulum hanging below it. The big hands moved with surprising speed and precision as he unwound the line from the holding board. He straightened out each kink that appeared in the line. The family trout hole ranged from forty to eight feet deep. Two islands marked its imaginary two-mile circumference. Each island was narrow; their rock points were aimed at each other about three quarters of a mile apart. Buster had explained to me that morning that the two islands were really connected by a ridge that ran about fifty feet deep. Lake trout as big as Chinook salmon fed along that deeply submerged reef. To catch them, the paddler had to move very slowly in a figure-eight pattern back and forth across the reef.

As we moved in the pattern, Grandfather could feel the lead weight touching the flanks of the deep reef. He would grunt and bring in the copper line with his right hand coiling it very carefully at his feet. We worked our way slowly into the wind. When he could no longer feel the weight hit along the bottom, he turned. "She goes down now," he said. We had already passed beyond the reef, so I turned to follow the imaginary line between that point and a point a hundred feet out from the shore of the island. As we did so, the wind caught us broadside, and I had to sweep heavily with the paddle to keep on the right path. We picked up speed just as Grandfather was swiftly dropping coils of copper line over the side to keep the KB down along the bottom, where the bigger lake trout would be feeding. "Nei, nei, Jeddy, slow, slow." I switched sides then and used a draw stroke to hold us on the imaginary line and slow us down at the same time. "Ja ja. Good. Is there." Arms straining, knees shoved against the ribs at the bottom, I inched our way toward the island as slow as I could. Grandfather sat up in the bow, his huge hand holding the copper line across the palm. He gently pumped his hand up and down to keep the KB working. He was staring at some point far away, saying nothing. Suddenly his hand shot down into the water. I heard him gasp at the weight of the strike and at the effort of trying to reseat himself.

The coils of line at his feet leaped and pulsed as more line went through his hand. I swung the canoe in a wide circle, with the line slanting down at a 45 degree angle defining a constant arc. With the slack in the line taken up, Grandfather could now reset the hook. He pumped his right arm up into the sky, grunting each time with the effort of heaving on the braided copper line. Then he began to bring up the line a foot at a time. "Big. Ja. Big." As he brought up the line with his right hand, his left coiled it in circles at his feet. Suddenly the line began to come in easily; too easily. "Quick, Jeddy. He come. Paddle hard." Apparently the big fish was running toward the pressure point above him. I turned the canoe; the wind caught us and extended the arc in a matter of seconds. "Ja, still there. Big." We slowed. The trout began pumping with heavy movements, forcing Grandfather's hand down in jerky movements as the line went out. "Go with him, Jeddy. Slow now."

The canoe, the line, and the fish moved in concert out to the deeper part of the lake. The fish continued to take line, and then gradually slowed. The line went straight down. We drifted into the big water, the islands now a mile to the rear. The canoe rose and fell as the big waves passed beneath us. I drew gently against the wind to slow the drift. Grandfather sat staring out over the open water as if he were no longer fishing. Then very gently he whispered, "Koom now, big fella." He began to lift the wire; his right hand trembling now with each tiny movement. He was bleeding where the line cut through the thick calluses on his hands. I circled very slowly about the line. The black waves were cresting and sighing as they lifted the figure in the bow. His arm moved smoothly as if part of some terribly significant ritual. "Careful. Soon he sees canoe. Then he runs again." The line no longer pointed straight down but traveled in short desperate arcs to the right, then to the left. "He goes." The line again pulled the coils at his feet. His left hand deftly prevented the leaping coils from tangling as the line shot out in spurts of several feet. I followed again with the canoe until he slowed, then stopped. The slow dance continued. We both ignored the waves as we stared down the line into the water. After another shorter run, I could see him, a huge silver shadow far down in the black water. He moved slowly in awkward arcs, first on one side, then the other. The fish was dying. I learned later that it was experiencing the effects of rapid decompression. Finally, his head pointed straight up to the canoe; as it came out of the water Grandpa hooked his fingers into the gills and lifted him into the canoe behind his seat. There was a thick piece of beaver-cut log on the bottom of the canoe. He picked it up and hit the fish on the head just behind the eyes. The fish quivered and lay still.

Grandfather's big, thick fingers were shaking slightly as he took his pipe out of the pocket of his wool shirt. "Ja, dots a goo-od fish. Vee go now." He nodded at the other canoe still making figure eights back at the two islands far off on the horizon. He lit the pipe, turned and looked for a long moment at the lake trout; then he let out the line again and rewrapped it on the holding stick. A tall, straight figure, he wore a black wool hat billed in the front after the fashion of loggers of his day. In his heavy suspenders, thick wool pants of nondescript color pegged at the cuff, and thick wool socks and moccasins, he seemed to belong in this place. It was if he had taken root here and taken on his weathered appearance at this very spot. He was a man of huge hands, few words, and shy smiles; he was now over sixty-five. This was to be his last trip for fall trout.

Over the next few days, hundreds of pounds of trout were cleaned and rubbed down with salt, and carefully packed in extra big Duluth packs. First, the pack was soaked in the lake and then lined with a thick layer of sphagnum moss. A layer of fish would be added and then another layer of wet moss. When the pack was full, we tied it off. I followed Buster as he carried one of the packs back to the cool dark swamp. He grunted with the weight of it as he hung it on a stout branch. "The wind catches it up there and evaporates the water," he explained. "Keeps it cool just like in the icehouse at home." The packs were wetted down several times a day.

On the third night, after supper, Hank asked, " What do you think, Pa—we got enough?" Most of the decisions were actually stated by Hank. But, like the others, this one seemed to present a consensus already formed. "Ja, ja. Ve got plenty. Maybe go home now." Buster started to walk over to his personal pack. "What the hell, might as well finish what's left of this bottle of brandy." Hank and Junior drifted over in that direction. "Yes sir-ee," he continued. "That stuff is too heavy to carry. I got a lit bit in my pack, too. No use taking it home." As the two bottles traveled around the circle, the talk became more animated. Hank was usually quiet spoken and spent more time listening than talking. A bottle seemed to open up some hidden place for him, and before you knew it you might find yourself in a one-armed bear grip around your shoulder, listening to stories he needed to tell. His voice was high and coming very fast now, "No bears here. Remember that goddamn bear last spring, Bus, when we were beaver trapping?" Hank giggled and pounded Bus on the shoulder, "Yeah, I'll never forget him. We even left the tent flaps tied back so he could walk right in. Know what he did? That son of a bitch cut a hole through the back of my new tent." Hank was beside himself with glee, laughing and waving the bottle of brandy. "Should've seen the look on ole Bus's face when we came back to camp that night. That bear had piled all the stuff that he didn't like into the frying pan. Just as neat as you please, stacked up cans like you was in a Safeway store. Yeah, he didn't like beans. Put a tooth hole through each can then stacked it up in the frying pan. We had to go all the way into town the next day to get more grub." The wind was coming up and pointing sheets of flame at the long shadows that ran along the ground and up the tree trunks. "Bus looked for that bear for a couple of days when we got back. He never showed up again."

The talk turned to hunting and then back to bears. My uncles spoke of another trip where the whole family had gone out for some recreational fishing. They camped on an island in a country frequented by large numbers of tourists, and bears in about equal numbers. The bears in North Bay on Basswood Lake are some of the world's most highly educated. Over the years, they have worked out this technique where they wait at night for the tourists to get into their tents and until their fire is almost out. Then one or two bears saunter into the camp. They knock over a few things to let people know that guests have arrived. At this point, there is a lot of running around. Mainly, people are trying to get away from the bears by jumping into their canoes. There is a lot of shouting and such as they paddle around out in the lake safe from the bears. The bears roam around the campsite at will, laying in on the tourists' giant supply of store-bought groceries.

Imagine the surprise of the two bears that swam out to the island where our family was camped. They were greeted by men swarming out of the tents firing illegal pistols of many different calibers, and women throwing firecrackers. Now, the bears knew that this was just a game and that it was really their island, so in the time-honored fashion, they ran back into the dark trees to wait until all of the noise died down. But the family did not play that game, and instead they got out a half dozen flashlights and two bottles of booze. They hounded those poor bruins from pillar to bush firing their guns, yelling and pounding on the trees with sticks. Finally, the bears, with what little dignity they could muster, took to the water. Even then, the family got into their canoes and hounded them all the way to the mainland, singing obscene songs and hitting them with sticks.

Sonny and I left the circle around the fire and went back to the tent, falling asleep to the sound of laugher mixed with the sound of the wind flapping the sides of the tent. I wakened in the dark tent to the sounds of battle. It was all around us. There were moans mixed with shouts, and in the background, deep-felt snoring. The sound rose and fell, but did not go away. I could pick out Bus's voice in the tumult, shouting, "Oh, oh, uh," then falling off into piteous moans and groans, only to rise again later. Hank was shouting the commands, "They're coming. They're over here. Get 'em! " I found our flashlight, and Sonny and I crawled over the combatants. The light hit Junior's face and I could see that his eyes were open and staring. "Sorry, Uncle Junior, didn't mean to . . ." Then I stopped, for I could hear him softly snoring, his gaze fixed on some spot on the roof of the tent. Sonny and I found a spot under the canoes that was out of the wind. In the distance, we could hear the rumble of heavy artillery and shouts of battle as our uncles prepared themselves for the morrow.

Grandfather was up first. As he came to get water from the lake, he laughed at our sleepy countenances. "You no like music when you sleep?" We broke camp in record time. There was very little talking as we loaded the canoes. The wind was heavy and carried a light rain as the two heavily loaded canoes worked their way back through the islands of La Croix. The rain did not let up as we motored up the Nina Moose River. Mallards jumped straight up out of the fall-colored reeds before flying off at great speed. It was an incredible trick to watch: it looked like they had leaped up on a platform four feet above the water and then launched into flight from there.

Slowly, the talking began. Partridge season would come soon, and then duck and deer hunting season, which gave the men much to discuss. The teasing and joshing picked up. The closer we got to our truck on the Echo Trail, the greater the activity level. It was dark when Sonny and I crawled under the tarp in the back of the truck. I watched the black silhouettes of tree tops sliding by in an endless band. The two canoes on the overhead rack thundered accompaniment as the trucks roared over the dirt road. Much later, the first tavern appeared. It was set in a swamp far back from the road, marked only by a small electric sign on top of it. A huge box-like structure, it had only three cars parked alongside it. I vaguely heard the slam of the truck doors. "Kid, you want anything? A couple beers and we're on our way." I didn't answer. "Naw, Bus, he's asleep. So is Sonny." I heard the crunch of boots on gravel, and then their pounding up the wooden stairs. Far away, a door opened and released a spurt of jukebox music that faded again when the door closed. I was awakened again by flashlights and voices. "Sorry kid. God, look at the size of those trout! Lac La Croix, huh?" Hank, leaning forward with his bottle of beer. "Hell Bus, take that one . . . yeah, the big one there. We got lots more. You too, Luke. Got all we need for winter. Ain't that right, Bus?" The voices and flashlights disappeared, and I was left with the thick smell of fish, wet moss, and the smoky smell from the rain tarp covering the back of the pickup.

Throughout the night there were more lights and other voices. Again, the prideful ritual of the fish, the awed voices, and the giving. The family made its triumphant tour of every swamp tavern from the Echo Trail to Ely, and from there to Robinson Lake. The stories grew longer and the voices louder. The closing of the last tavern coordinated nicely with the emptying of the last fish pack. At Robinson Lake, each cabin had its kerosene lamp in the window. Our log house was the last one. "Night, kid," said Uncle Hank, and Buster drove up the road.

I never really heard just how my uncles explained that fall trout trip. I knew that things were very quiet for days, as they usually were after some particularly outrageous deed. There were a lot of sly smiles among the men. When intercepted by the women, who felt wronged by the whole affair, such a smile would be quickly impaled by a dour look. There were many screen doors fixed. Roof leaks, unattended for months, were suddenly repaired. Saws were sharpened. Waist-high grass was scythed. After a week or two, the mood softened and the stories could be told at the dinner table. The women giggled behind their hands, still disapproving but participating according to family rules laid down long ago. Things went on, as they always had.

The web that provided support and yet constrained each of us to remain in our individual role was in play again. Each family member felt supported and sustained by the web. But if you stayed, there were only a very limited set of options. Up to this point, there were only one or two persons who had left the basin and struck out on their own.

2

The Family at Robinson Lake

The nine houses at Robinson Lake defined the family's boundaries. They were sprayed out in a lopsided pattern along the shores of two lakes. Most of the houses were clustered around the smaller lake, because that is where the train stopped. Mallards loved the small lake, too. In the fall, the lake stood shoulder high in wild rice. A few years prior to my grandfather's arrival at the basin, Indians had lived there. They also thought the small lake was pretty special. They had left one of their birch bark canoes down in the north end which had apparently been used to harvest the wild rice. The bow had been smashed, probably by a falling tree. A small boy could use that canoe by sitting so far back in the stern that the shattered bow hung just above the water.

The two lakes were connected by a stream. Each of the families had built their house on a small hill. There were also tiny islands each surrounded by swamp. The swamps varied a good deal in character and in the tone that they set. There were the blueberry bogs pierced by tiny boreal spruce. The bogs were thick, springy, and moist even at the end of summer. The swamp that connected the two lakes was like a huge savanna, with grass higher than your head. In the spring, the bog would be cut by deep veins of brown water that the northern pike followed as they came up to spawn. We spent hours laying on our bellies trying to catch a pike with our hands but none of us had a sensitive enough touch or the patience required to actually catch one that way.

Next to our log cabin down by the big lake, there was a small swamp choked with alder trees. This swamp contained saplings of every conceivable dimension, and constantly renewed itself. I never really thought of it as a swamp; for a young boy, the place was more like a shopping mall. It satisfied ever-present needs for tent poles, rafting poles, fishing poles, and crotched saplings for making slingshots.

A railroad track neatly bisected the pattern of swamps and houses and gave the community a sense of coherence it would not have otherwise had. The ostensible purpose of the track was to transport iron ore from the local mines in Ely to the shipping ports on Lake Superior, a hundred miles to the south and east. However, from our viewpoint, the tracks were a personal footpath, placed there solely for our convenience. A brisk walk of a half-mile would take you within shouting distance of every house in Robinson Lake. Grandpa Nicholson had built the roadbed and set the tracks at the turn of the century. That fact validated our sense that the tracks belonged to the family. A significant part of the second generation made their living maintaining those tracks.

The store, presided over by Grandma, was at the center of the village. From time to time, she would change the location, but each of the tiny houses built for her always included a room with a counter and some shelves. From a boy's point of view, the basic function of the store was to provide an endless supply of candy bars and an icebox full of cold pop. During the hot summer months, a vague odor of chocolate always hung over the place. Her last store was the noblest of all. It sat high up on a knoll flanked by two huge White pines. The house itself was walled in by lilac bushes, with a garden in the back. It was a gathering point not only for the family, and for two hermits who lived back in the bush, but for anything that was newsworthy, which all eventually found its way to the store. The only telephone in the village was at Aunt Gladys's home which sat right next to the store. Answering the phone required that somebody run down the road a quar-

27

ter-mile to announce the call. This in turn required that the callee run a quarter-mile back, while the caller waited patiently on the other end. To this day, I feel mildly intimidated by telephone calls.

Nearly everyone in the family came up the tracks to the store at least once each day. Mainly we gave and received information, and made one or two purchases of things forgotten the previous day. If you were an adult, the ritual included at least one cup of coffee before leaving. "Morgan, Jeddy," Grandma would say, as she slowly descended the two steps from her kitchen. "Alleece, her cold iss better?" Grandma was not tall, but she comes to the mind as a large, square, powerful figure. Always neat and clean with fresh apron and a vague odor of lilac, she had fine features and bore herself as if she had once been a great beauty, which was indeed the case. She had piercing blue eyes, but wore her graying hair in a bun. Grandma was the epicenter about which the entire community revolved. The store never made a profit, it was her way of continuously giving to the entire family. A chronic shortage of money could somehow be balanced by endless credit from the store.

Her greetings were accompanied by a smile, a head nod, and a careful appraisal. Grandpa would look down from the kitchen door, smile, and say, "Leet bit coffee?" The coffee came from an enormous pot that occupied a permanent position at the rear of the wood stove. Grandpa liked his coffee thick, so the grounds were only thrown out once a week. New grounds were added to the old ones each day, and water added for re-boiling.

If some member of a household did not make an appearance at the store, a messenger would be sent to find out what was wrong. An illness would produce a flurry of activity along the track that invariably included Grandma's huge figure flying along, wrapped in her thick black coat and her cane tapping along on the ties as she went. The oversized purse slung from the strap at her shoulder carried her emergency kit with everything that the family could probably need, ranging from money to aspirin to a loaf of bread. Other family members would follow and do whatever else was needed.

Grandma's flying inspection visits even included Aunt Fanny on her sick days. Aunt Fanny had worked out a way of standardizing illness; instead of having the flu or a cold sneak up on her unawares, she had legislated that all of her illness would fall on Wednesdays. She gave the whole ritual an even more majestic ring by decreeing that Wednesday was her sick day. This meant that there would be absolutely no demands upon her during that day. A request to go berry picking or to help with the canning would be summarily dealt with by a firm, "No, I can't do that. That is my sick day, you know." All of this was accompanied by a great deal of eye contact and stern expression. Dissenting voices—and these were few—would be referred back to Grandmother. She protected Aunt Fanny and her sick days as strenuously as everyone else in the family. Each of us ended up feeling that we owed Grandma a great deal just by way of the protection, if for no other reason. There was practically nothing that she could request that would not be done willingly and quickly. If you were a young child, the payment for helping could be a penny candy; for older members it was, "Tusen takk."

She seldom expressed displeasure, although when she did its effect could be devastating. I remember a winter day when she discovered that I had not sawed enough wood for my mother on the previous day. She stood in the doorway of her kitchen, her level gaze fixed on me, shaking her head. "Not be real man," she said. With that, she closed the door and left me standing there, absolutely crushed. Her words still come to me at those precise moments when I'm inclined to whisper to myself, "Oh hell, that is good enough for now."

The only one who seemed impervious to Grandma's displeasure was an acid-tongued uncle who married into the family and then moved to Wyoming. He carried about him that sense of certainty that seems to come only to football coaches and tenured professors. He was an example of the former, and by definition the only educated person in the family. He knew that in the divine eventual order of things, only college graduates would be considered worthy. Being able to survive a blizzard or track a deer had nothing to do with the world of symbols, prizes, and power that he was familiar with. He was my first contact with that part of society that believes that being a good person or highly skilled at what you do is not all that important. From his pinnacle of privilege, people were not classified based on what they actually did, but on what they were driving. It didn't matter whether or not clothes protected you from the cold, but what brand they were and where you bought them. Eventually he became an important functionary for a large oil company in Venezuela.

Like a visitation of the plague, once a year he would bring his family to Robinson Lake. Each visit was anticipated with dread because no one possessed the verbal skills to put him in his place. And none of the men were allowed to correct the process in their usual ways. In Grandma's pantheon, Franklin D. Roosevelt was a hero of mythic proportions; his picture hung in the kitchen in the position of prominence right over the water pail. The visiting uncle was a deeply rooted conservative and he expressed his views at great length in irritable argument. The family managed to accept his deviation from manners in good grace because of the shortness of his visits. But I do remember Grandma's purple-cheeked disbelief once when FDR's picture had been found hanging on the wall of the outhouse!

For those of us going to school in Ely, nine miles away, the store was also our bus terminal. Each day a small group of us would gather in glum silence in front of Grandma's living room window and watch for the school bus. That way, no one had to stand out in the snow in twenty below zero as a price tag for becoming educated. Later, when one by one the boys left Robinson Lake for the war, each in his turn sat by the same window to wait for a Greyhound bus that would take him to where the action was happening. Grandma was not a hugger, nor did I ever see her kiss anyone. But as each of us prepared to leave, she would stand directly in front of us—standing very close—and look us right in the eye. "Here, take dis for coffee on the way." With that she would stuff a ten-dollar bill in our shirt pocket and then turn and quickly leave the room so that we would not see the tears.

Growing up in a wilderness community meant that there were no fences and there were no music lessons because there were no teachers. There was no little league; nobody played soccer. There were no organized competitions of any kind. Uncles and older cousins taught you what you needed to know when the need arose. We were not taught any of the usual spectator sports. It was not because anyone had anything against those skills, but stick and ball games were simply irrelevant in our lives. Academic skills were viewed in pretty much the same light. Someone might notice or comment if you couldn't read or do numbers, but other than that academic skills were not particularly important. None of us were outstanding students, getting high grades was just not part of the family program.

Each day, we put in the requisite amount of time addressing the neverending lists that adults seem to have in mind for non adults. There was wood we had to chop, pile, and bring in. There were things we had to paint, scrap, haul, and stack. There were errands we needed to run. Once completed, however, the rest of the day was our own, we were free to find our own paths. My younger brother Mike and my two cousins, Sonny and Ray, formed a group to exploit this free time. There were no schedules other than the requirement to be home for supper. There was a sense of unlimited possibility and unlimited time. As a group we set our own goals and identified our own projects. There was no adult present the spring we raised the ancient Indian birch bark canoe out of the mud of little Robinson Lake. There was no adult present when we built the tree house thirty feet off the ground in a great Norway pine, complete with a stove that worked and a flag that could be raised from inside. In these various enterprises, we were a cohesive group that worked cooperatively. We modeled ourselves pretty much after the adult members of the community, and we understood that as a group we could accomplish far more than any single individual on his own.

Spring was initiated on the first warm day after the ice left the lake. A small group of boys would slip around the point where adults could not see what was happening. The group would wade out knee-deep on the slippery bottom and stand there with the legs turning a dull blue, talking bravely all the while. Finally, someone would take a deep breath and dive. The water was like a physical blow that forced each of us to porpoise up out of the water. The swim consisted of as much disconnected kicking and arm thrashing as you could get done on one breath of air. Later, when hearing of this, the adults would shake their heads and cluck their tongues. They smiled as they did so because many of them had done exactly the same thing in the same spot when it had been their turn inside the magic bubble.

As a group, we moved in an aura of invulnerability. The bubble moved with us. It was not magic in any formal organized sense, it was created by play that shifted back and forth between what is real and what is not. Stories told by adults in the village and books read at school became group play, and would follow a course that might last an hour, a day, or for the entire summer. Our playground was the lake basin which had a diameter of about three miles. There were only one or two trails; we preferred to make our own. Essentially, we were trying to learn to move across the country and connect with a lake three miles away or a ridge two miles to the south. We would carefully put a blaze mark on trees spaced about sixty feet apart, marking both sides so we could find our way back. We would work for several days on a project like this. There was a special pleasure in finding our own path into a tiny lake several miles away, and real excitement when we would first see sunlight coming off the water and know that we did it right.

Sometimes we would carry camping gear to one of the lakes and stay up most of the night fending off imaginary bears. We pretended not to notice that, invariably, one or two adults would just happen to drop by our camp that night or the next day.

On one of our forays, we walked four miles into old Purvis's place. He wasn't there. We started back along the old logging trace road that wound its way through the big swamp. I thought we could do better by going in a straight line right across the swamp to Robinson Lake. We had no compass, the fiction being that only a tourist needed a compass to tell them where North was. We did have my single-shot 10 gauge that was choked down so much it fired more like a rifle than a shotgun. As we headed through the big swamp, the clouds came in. A misty rain started falling, dampening our spirits considerably. By late afternoon, the idea of forging a new path began to lose its charm. By the end of the day, it was four very wet Robinson Rangers that began looking for a place to camp for the night. We began scouting for a big spruce tree that would keep off most of the rain and let us build a fire.

While searching for the tree, we encountered a spruce hen sitting high up on a branch. The hammer on the old shotgun looked exactly like an old flintlock. You needed to pull it back two clicks to cock it. I aimed very carefully from a range of about sixty feet. The gun let off a tremendous roar, answered by a cloud of feathers where the bird had sat. Except for a pair of feet and some wing feathers, dinner had disintegrated. We sat in glum silence by a smoky fire when the engine of a freight train sounded not 500 yards away! We had missed Robinson Lake by a good mile. This is among the stories still told at Robinson Lake gatherings.

Some of the adults seemed to retain a sense of this bubble from their own childhoods; others did not. Several uncles did, as did my mother. A conversation while walking to the store could be interrupted at any time by her calling to crows flying by. She might stop to answer a loon sitting out in the middle of Robinson Lake. The wide range occupied by her conversations was taken as a matter of course by other family members. In fact, they would mention with no little pride that the birds often answered when she called. Sometimes she would get into a conversation with a loon several lakes away. After several exchanges you could hear the loon start up the hellishly long take-off run they require when they wish to become airborne. A few minutes later the loon would pass over and land in her lake.

She had that special child's sense of beauty, and a deep sense and about what was important and what was not. I have watched her hugging trees. I knew that she talked to them, and to flowers as well. All of this was done with a sense of joy in the sheer beauty of things, rather than in any dour confusion about whether birds and trees could actually talk.

Each spring required a group search for Martin's dugout canoe. His canoe was about sixteen feet long, made from a huge log he had hollowed out long ago. Old Martin was a trapper-hermit who had arrived at the lake basin about the same time as my grandfather. Each year the wind and ice tended to deposit it in unlikely places on Robinson Lake. It was our self-assigned task to take a lunch and a boat and cruise the shoreline of the lake until we found it.

Martin lived for a while at a point on the other side of Robinson Lake. He built well, both cabins and boats. His problem was that he tended to be a bit careless with his fires. Periodically, his stove would overheat, and the ensuing fire would totally demolish his home. Rather than rebuild, he would move to a different place and start all over again. A pile of burnt logs and a midden heap of old cans and snoose jars marked each spot.

The dugout canoe was elegantly shaped, worn by toil and water to be smooth to the touch, and seemingly indestructible. After reading about the Polynesians, we fitted it with outrigger pontoons and a square-rigged sail. It was our flagship for cruising the lake in search of adventures. If we needed money to go to town for a movie, it became our fishing dory while we trolled hand lines for northern pike, which we then sold to Uncle Hank for mink feed.

Without time schedules, and relatively free of adult supervision, the group could occasionally drift into activities of dubious merit. After seeing a movie with Errol Flynn as Robin Hood, we spent months constructing first bows and arrows and then cross bows of our own design. These latter were powered by thick rubber bands cut from inner tubes that pulled a carved wooden arrow along a slot at the top of the barrel. The arrows were tipped with empty small caliber cartridge cases. They could be aimed like a rifle. Armed in this fashion—dressed in green capes and carrying long wooden swords—we were a piteous scourge for partridge, squirrels, and rabbits for miles around.

Our intensive research into these matters convinced us that we needed heavier artillery which ultimately led to the development of our mobile cabbage cannon. The cannon had all of the speed and mobility of a French 75 artillery piece, and for our more limited objectives, was just as accurate. First, we cut rubber bands from inner tubes that were three feet long and several inches wide. Two ends of the rubbers were tied off on each side of a leather pouch. The other two ends of the tubes were tied off with rawhide loops. Two cousins held the loops while the cannoneer simply placed a cabbage or rutabaga in the pouch and walked backward. If a steady barrage was required, we tied the rawhide ends to two birch trees spaced about four feet apart. The well-trained cannoneer would know just how many steps to take in order to get the right distance, compensating all the while for the size and heft of the cabbage. The missile would soar off in a great looping trajectory for a range of a hundred yards or more. By putting the cannon holders up on a slight rise with the cannoneer below them, you could get a proper elevation. The cabbage would almost disappear into the heavens and then descend soundlessly into the waters of little Robinson Lake, where some dignified mallard duck might be having his noon luncheon of wild rice. When the cabbage hit the lake, there would be a huge water spout rising into the air. Under ordinary circumstances, a mallard can rise two or three feet straight up into the air and then fly off at a great speed. The cabbage cannon gave the whole performance an added intensity. I have always been able to understand a mallard's natural mistrust of small boys.

The ubiquitous cannon was tested against a wide range of targets. In mid-afternoon the turtles in little Robinson Lake climbed up on their favorite logs to sunbathe, gathering in clusters and clots like sunbathers on the beach. A well-aimed potato could lift a sunbathing turtle off his log and deposit him far out to sea. We were seldom able to get in more than two or three shots before the entire turtle colony would be in the water, with only their heads sticking out in mute protest.

Then reports came through the single telephone at the section house in Robinson Lake of a twilight cannonade of a resort owner's house several miles away. He had a firmly established history of being unfriendly to the interests of young boys; he had even posted his sand beach off limits to anyone other than the paying tourists. His report about the night attack was somewhat garbled by the fact that his English-speaking ability was limited, even when he was calm. He said that he had heard a thundering on his roof. He went out to discover a garden load of rotten vegetables whistling out of the gloom to drop on his house. He claimed to have been struck in mid-stride by a cabbage, but this was never documented. The matter led to a family council meeting and a speedy decision to retire the cannon from further use.

Occasionally the requirements of the season would make serious inroads into our unlimited freedom. The most noteworthy of these intrusions was the berry-picking season. There was some peculiar feature of this interval that brought out authoritarian elements in even the most benevolent of adults. Without hesitation, all the Robinson Lake adults could recall hours of berry picking toil under the most arduous of conditions. Their stories often included tragic tales of mosquito hordes, swamps, being lost, and being chased by bears. Their faces would grow stern when they spoke of such things. The drop in their voices meant that these were indeed stories to be taken seriously. Making things difficult at the end of the day they would measure how much you had picked and compared it against what they themselves remembered picking. In these lopsided comparisons, the new generation was always found lacking.

The call would come out from the command post at the store that the pin cherries were ripe, or the strawberries were coming in along the right of way by the tracks. Each message sent a shudder through the community of captive berry pickers. The blueberry session lasted for weeks. Boys and girls as young as six or seven would be dispatched down the tracks, five pound coffee can in hand, to the bogs in some years or the ridges on others. All of the uncles in the village mysteriously disappeared at this time, called to activities unknown.

If indeed there were a social season at Robinson Lake, its apogee would have to be Fourth of July, the one time of the year that there would be a mass exodus of the entire family to the town of Tower twelve miles to the south. Forty years before, Tower had been the lumbering capitol of northern Minnesota; however, all the big pine had been cut, profits from its celebrated status had ended. What was left of the town relied upon the iron ore mines and the summer tourists drawn to nearby Lake Vermillion.

Tower's downtown section was thinly spread along both sides of the state highway. It started and stopped in about six blocks. One or two buildings still had those two-story false fronts that you see in films of western saloons. They were holdovers from the logging days. On Main Street, there was one of everything; one hardware store, one grocery store, one barber shop, one beauty shop, one garage, and one restaurant. The only thing that broke the symmetry of the city planning was the fact that half of the stores were taverns. The original inhabitants had worked it out neatly so that they alternated; liquor store, one of the other kind, liquor store, one of the other kind, and so forth. The fact that there were no trees along the street made it easy to find the kind of store that you had in mind.

A month before the Fourth of July, anticipatory quivers of excitement ran through the community of Tower. Town leaders made arrangements to bring a renowned politician in to give a speech. This led to the need for a platform right there on Main Street. Somebody also had to arrange with the local Indian reservation for dancers to come in and perform. For their partiuclar kind of dancing, timing was of the essence. Early in the day, there would be a lot of Indians who were good dancers. But as the day wore on, there would be a lot who felt like dancing but whose abilities could no longer keep pace with their enthusiasm.

For young men of adventurous spirit there were the races. Boys would begin to practice for these events early in the summer: sack races, forty-yard dashes, and relay races. At Robinson Lake, we would measure off what was thought to be forty yards and make short fierce sprints down the tracks. There was much speculation about what first and second prizes would be each year.

During the Fourth of July, the most conspicuous member of Robinson Lake was my father. To be fair, the man was conspicuous in almost any situation. He stood well over six feet tall, had jet black hair, and a smile that released a full set of white teeth. He looked like a movie star; but his local reputation was built less on good looks than on his abiding commitment to convivial gatherings. If a gathering was not to be found, he would often create one. He had quite naturally gravitated to the ranks of the Tower Marching Band. Tall and slim in his blue uniform with white piping, he took the position of bass drummer, and set the beat for the whole group. At football games or band competitions, you could always pick him out with his big grin, drumsticks moving in continuous circles.

The powerful economic forces of the Great Depression had

lifted my father and our family right out of the small community we lived in on the Dakota prairies. He had been the manager of a Bell Telephone office and active member of the business community. He had committed some unforgivable act that led to a public auction of all the furnishings in our home, and also necessitated one long, hot trip. The train brought us to my mother's birthplace and the family living in the lake basin in the Northern Minnesota wilderness. He never quite fit in to the community. He never stopped dreaming and never stopped working at two or more jobs, as a means of lifting us out of poverty. For years, there was no time left to spend with children and it was only my youngest brother Kim who ever really got close to Dad. None of us ever learned what had actually happened to him in the Dakota prairies so long ago.

The Fourth of July was special. For Dad, it meant the uniform had to be dry-cleaned. It also meant a very long day. Early in the morning the entire band would be taken in a thirty foot launch around the shores of Lake Vermillion. At each stopping place, they would serenade the inhabitants and then move on the next resort. They were to return by mid-day for the grand finale: the march down Tower's Main Street. This would formally launch the festivities.

We were all up early that morning. Mother was hunched over the kerosene lamp that sat on the kitchen table. She used the lamp to heat her hair irons. Her blonde hair was done up in tight rolls. She had a pinched look on her face as she worked out what it was that she would wear. She sent me across the tracks to her sister Norma's house to borrow a special pair of earrings. My brother Mike followed soon after in a quest for a red purse. Finally, she went over herself to get something that she could not ask us to get. This time Norma returned with her to borrow something from mother. Dad took off early in the pickup truck, with the drum sitting up next to him in the front seat.

The entire family was scurrying up and down the tracks or

39

driving in and out. The problem was to figure out who was riding with Uncle Hugo. Who would take Grandma and Grandpa? Contingency plans were made as to who would take the women home if the men launched into a full-scale weekend party. All of us were dressed in freshly laundered cotton shirts, the kind we usually wore to school or to church. Each of us carried all of the money we had been able to earn from berry picking. Our hair was freshly combed. We had barely been able to get Mother to agree to let us wear our fastest tennis shoes instead of the dress-up kind. We stamped back and forth from one parked car to another, hoping that we could get an early ride. The uncles, dressed in slacks and fancy shoes that only came out of the closet for Easter and Christmas, sat around smiling and talking back and forth in a real quiet way. Finally, the women came out, to the appreciative comments of the men waiting outside. Soon after, the safari of pickup trucks and vintage sedans was under way.

According to the schedule, the launch containing Tower's prideful marching band should by now have returned from circling Lake Vermillion. When we arrived, the parade had not yet started. We practiced sprints and looked over the competition from the local Tower boys and the Indian boys from the nearby reservation. Eventually people began drifting down to the dock on the Vermillion River to look for the launch. It came around the corner just as we arrived. Trim and white with little flags waving from the shiny brass stanchions fitted to the bow, the boat moved steadily to the docking area. However, there was a strange lack of movement; no one on the boat was waving. There was no music announcing the boat's triumphant arrival. The driver slowed the engine and the boat drifted sideways to the dock. Instruments and bodies lay spread about the back of the boat. There were a few feeble efforts to move, to stand, to pick up instruments, but not much real progress. Buster nodded his head. "Your dad said at each place they stop, people usually offer them a drink after they play. Must have been more places to play this year."

The crowd was dead silent, as if the sheer magnitude of the event was too much to even comment upon. They stood back as the band slowly emerged from the boat and formed up on the dock. White shirts no longer freshly laundered, hats askew, and jackets unbuttoned, they were anything but Tower's fast-stepping, prize-winning marching band. My father stared straight ahead as he laid out a slow beat for the march to town. The crowd strung out behind them. The beat picked up as they moved into Main Street. They came around the corner with a bit of flair. As they came abreast of the first bar, the crowd standing outside waved the marchers in through the door. The procedure was unplanned and unpracticed, but the band never paused. They marched right out the back door and up the alley to the rear entrance of the next saloon. People commented on the gradual loss of structure and coherence to the band. The marching theme became hard to follow. The tightly planned schedule for the events became difficult to find, but no one seemed to mind. No medals were won in the races that year. Several uncles did not make it home for three days.

Deer season was a tremendous time of year to be a boy in Robinson Lake. By about age twelve, boys could be usefully employed as "drivers" on the family deer hunts. We had to wait until adolescence before becoming one of the riflemen. This was not a sport. Individuals who were reliable shooters were highly valued. A well-made gun was regarded as a thing of real beauty. The idea was to lay in as much meat as possible for the entire village. The meat was divided equally among all of the families. Actually, we fed on deer meat all year long. While the game wardens suspected this was the case, only one family member had ever been caught, and that was due to a faulty strategy on his part. On one occasion, the wardens were so sure that there was illegal deer meat in Grandma's house that they came with a warrant. They could smell the meat but could not find it. The story was that Grandma had put the partially cooked roast in her basket of fresh laundry.

There were a few inches of snow on the ground and the lakes

had been frozen over for some time. The fall was the first time I had the opportunity to be one of the shooters. About a dozen uncles and cousins planned to spread out and drive through the big swamp on the north end of the lake. Three of us would be waiting up on the ridge. Very early one morning, we collected in the living room and kitchen of our cabin. Henry looked at Buster, "Bus, I'll take Pa and Jer across the lake. We'll circle and come in behind the ridge. Give us about a half hour lead before you start."

My Grandpa, Uncle Buster, and I moved quickly across the lake. It was dark and it was very cold—the kind of cold where your boots squeak each time you take a step. There was little talking. The moon had been down for some time, so the shoreline looked almost black. The end of the high ridge tucked into a bay at the end of the lake creating a gently sloping rock that we could walk up to get up on the ridge itself. There was very little brush. We worked our way about a half-mile along the ridge before the eastern horizon began to glow a dull red. We began to see the outlines of the two gullies reaching up from the darkened cedar swamp immediately below us. Far away across the lake, we could hear a screen door slam.

Henry placed me on the ridge where I had a clear view of one of the gullies that ran up its side. He and Grandpa continued on along the ridge somewhere near the second gully. I stood leaning against a Norway pine and listened to the sound of their footsteps in the snow. It was getting lighter. Very slowly, a black mass below me emerged as a large rock. Black trunks became gray. Then it was light enough so you tell birch from poplar. Night had changed to day so slowly and with such subtleness you could not really find the point where it was one and not the other. About a half mile away, down by the lakeshore I could hear the sounds of the drive beginning. Here, the sound of a stick banging against a tree trunk, there a voice.

I had been told to stand very still because the deer see movement more than they see color. I slid the 30–06 bolt action rifle from my shoulder and concentrated on the sounds. It was bitterly cold. The bottoms of my feet were the first to detect it, as the cold reached up through inner soles and wool socks. The line of sound down in the swamp moved steadily toward me. Nobody was shooting. I stood against the tree, trying not to move my head as I watched for motion. Generally, the deer would slip through the trees several hundred yards ahead of the drivers. The drivers were close enough now so that I could hear Mike's voice far off to the left. Then I caught a glimpse of a gray shadow moving from one clump of trees to another. There was no sound, just this form that appeared and reappeared as it moved out of the gully and up the hill. The young buck had his head down as if it were playing a game of hide and seek. I dropped my mitten to the ground, and threw the rifle to my shoulder. He saw the movement and began his run. He seemed to move up and down as much as he moved forward. I tracked his movement for a brief moment then fired. I fired again just as he disappeared behind a small hill. During those few seconds I was totally focused, centered. There were no thoughts, just images. It is the same focus that you have when you run rapids in a canoe. It is the same absolute centeredness you have when you ski the powder snow in the trees. Everything happens much too quickly for thoughts to take control.

I ran over to the small hill. The buck lay there in the snow already dead. There was shouting from the left again, and then I heard the distinct sound of Grandpa's 45–70, first one shot that was joined by two shots from a different rifle. More shouting, then the whole company came charging up the hill. They were shouting, laughing, everyone talking at once. Somebody built a fire to make coffee. There were two deer to be cleaned. The ropes came out of the packs or from where they were carried tied around the waist. While still warm, the deer's front legs were tied off up over its head. With three of us to a rope, the deer on its back could then be pulled, toboggan fashion, back to the village.

Each fall, a giant rack would be built with birch logs and

stood next to the woodhouse. The deer would hang there while the meat seasoned. We would start each winter with the rack filled.

I received my first rifle for my tenth birthday. I carried it with me while bringing spring water down from the hill. The trip often produced a partridge and, in my fantasies, a lot more than that. Dad was one of the few people in the village that could hit anything flying with a shotgun. It was Hank who could hit a running deer. Some of us carried pistols, but none of us were very good with them. A box of twenty-two shells might produce three or four partridge. Every now and then, Hank would bring out his 45 Colt pistol and shame us all with the fact that we could not hit anything with it. The only saving grace was that Hank couldn't hit anything, either. Nobody in Robinson Lake could afford the thousand rounds required to be an expert with such a gun. Every year, the impossible pistol would be reverently returned to its special place in the gun cabinet. The only time it was used for anything was when a black bear got to chasing Hank's hunting dog around and around his house. Everyone agreed that it was pretty unusual bear behavior. But it irritated Hank enough for him to run upstairs and take the impossible pistol down. He stood with it on the bottom step of the porch. When the bear came by in hot pursuit of the frantic hunting dog, Hank shot it dead. Unfortunately, given that the range was only about ten feet, the deed did not add to his reputation as a pistolero.

By December, the snow would be piled up to the eaves of our tiny cabin down at the lake. Christmas set off a well-ordered sequence of events. It would begin with a gentle suggestion from Mother that maybe Mike and I should start looking for the right tree. That last phrase was always given special emphasis. Mother was seldom unreasonable about anything, but her expectations about Christmas were an exception to that rule. There was something about the holiday that reached deep inside her. For that day, everything must be perfect, and a perfect day must include a perfect tree. It was up to Mike and me to clomp around in the swamps and ridges on snowshoes in search of this perfection. With some minor distortions here and there, it wasn't too much trouble to imagine ourselves as two knights clad in layers of woolens off in search of the Holy Grail. Now the North Woods is not an orderly place. There is no one out there trimming these little spruce or pine trees, as nature doesn't care about absolute symmetry. We ran across plenty of trees that had fine tops, but slender bottoms, or fine bottoms, but a squirrelly top.

Mike and I would set up a pack for the axe and saw. Mother would slip in her bribe: several peanut butter sandwiches made with her home-baked brown bread. We both had bearpaw snowshoes, short enough so we could walk through thick underbrush. The harness for the snowshoes was made of old silk stockings, which tied easily and didn't freeze stiff like leather. The trouble with bear paws is that you have to swing your leg way out to the side, with each step because they are so wide. You don't have to do that for the long slender Chippewa frames, but they are harder to maneuver in thick brush. So Mike and I would set off across the lake, swaying from side to side like two penguins, in search of the perfect tree.

At the end of the day's odyssey we would return, each with a candidate tree. The two trees were placed in the snow bank by the front door for her inspection. She would appear at the door with a scarf wrapped around her head and stand up on the porch as if troops were passing in review. Mike and I were always careful to present the best possible features of our respective trees. There would be a long moment of silence while this great companion on fishing trips, this enthusiastic participant in sunsets and changing fall colors, found one flaw after another in our offerings. To my best recollection, we never did meet her standards. Sometimes there would be six or eight trees standing in silent protest before her door. The door would open and she would inevitably find the fatal flaw in each one of them. They just did not look like the trees in the pictures. Finally, it was not perfection that prevailed, but pity. After the third or fourth trip, her resolve would soften, and she would finally permit me to drill a few holes in the trunk of a less than perfect specimen. I would insert the necessary branches so skillfully that from across the room, the face-lift would blend in. The tree would be allowed in the house.

As the preparations proceeded, there would be one more trip into the swamp on snowshoes. This time it was to collect packsacks full of cedar and white pine boughs. These were used to make thick Christmas wreaths that were hung all over the house and sent as gifts to friends.

The women participated in the ritual of baking Christmas bread, Yule Kakka. Each of them had a slightly different way of baking this special bread. Young boys became connoisseurs of the subtle differences produced by adding various kinds of jellied fruits and nuts to the dough. The perfect bribe for a young boy was a two-inch-thick slice of freshly baked bread that was still warm enough to melt the pool of butter and peanut butter.

Shopping meant riding the train on the nine-mile trip to Ely, or trying to catch a ride in one of the cars in the village. Mysterious packages arrived by mail and disappeared to not be seen again until Christmas Eve. The three-room log cabin we lived in was too small to hide anything for very long. I always considered it a violation of children's rights that mother would stoop to hiding the presents in Grandma's woodshed.

My father always did his shopping on the very last day. He would arrive home late that afternoon with a carload of other family shoppers. These men had worked out their own eminently functional shopping ritual, as Ely is built on a slope, they would start at the top of the hill at Skala's Bar to build up their enthusiasm for the task at hand. From there, it was all downhill. They alternated with a store, then a bar, then a store, until they were picked up by one of the family cars and returned to Robinson Lake.

He would return from this annual expedition with eyes flashing and an armload of enormous packages, all gift wrapped. The children who met him at the door included my mother. Once she moved past the perfect tree barrier, Christmas worked an irresistible spell upon her. Each year there was a special gift for her from my father. He waited until the last minute to get it in order to heighten the suspense.

On the final day, there was much to be done. All the family members put on their finest clothes in preparation for the Christmas dinner at Grandma's house. This also included the requisite bath, the bath water of which came right out of Robinson Lake. The problem was to get through the three feet of ice to where the water lay. Mike and I would shovel off a patch of snow on the ice that was closest to the house. Then we would take turns chopping a hole about three feet in diameter often down on our knees, creating a basin. Chips the size of dinner plates would be strewn all over the snow. It was hot, sweaty work. Finally, when we could chop no further with the axes, we'd pull out the ice chisel mounted on a six foot shaft. One sharp rap with the chisel would pierce the bottom of the ice crater. The first glimpse of the water was always black; but as it flowed into the crater, it would transform into the familiar coffee-colored water of Robinson Lake. Pails of water were carried to the washtub sitting on top of the woodstove in the kitchen. Step one in the ritual Christmas bath was under way.

Finally, everyone was ready. The presents were in a box on a sleigh. Hair still damp, white shirts, sweaters, wool pants and shoe pacs with rubber bottoms and leather tops were standard. Add wool coats, thick hats, and chopper mitts with wool liners, and we were ready for the trip to Grandma's house on the hill. It to was often 10–20° below zero. Usually there was no wind. The smoke from wood fires marked the site of each of the nine houses. The smoke rose in pencil-thin white lines for hundreds of feet straight up in the air. Clouds of stars punctuated a jet-black sky. The contact of boots on snow gave off the squeaking sound that meant cold, very cold. The air burned our faces and throats as we took brief shallow breaths. During the walk, all sensations seemed to be

47

heightened. The sound of a door slamming a half-mile away was crisp and clear. It meant that Norma, Frank, and their son Norman were on their way, too. Voices of family converging upon the store were so clear that the speakers could be identified. Small groups, each pulling their sleighs, formed lines converging on one central place, all under bright stars that seemed very close by.

The store, the adjoining kitchen, and the dining room were filled with family. The women had on the dresses that they wore to church. However, it was the men who looked much different on Christmas night. Most of them seldom went to church, so they had little practice in wearing white shirts, let alone putting on ties. With their faces scrubbed red and their hair combed, I hardly recognized some of my uncles. Only Grandpa seemed at ease with the white shirt, black wool pants, and black vest with huge gold watch chain. He led small groups of men out to his woodshed. They returned to the steaming kitchen with faces slightly redder, casting sheepish grins to their spouses who were working in the kitchen with Grandma. She and her crew prepared the traditional six-course Norwegian Christmas dinner.

The most salient feature of this part of the evening was the overwhelming odor of lutefisk. In the kitchen, presided over by Grandma's square presence, each of the women worked over the dishes they had prepared. There were spare ribs, lutefisk, great mountains of mashed potatoes, and countless bowls of canned vegetables. The small boys would steer away from the latter as best they could. There were three or four platters of homemade bread, each baked by a different artist. For dessert, a table in the back of the kitchen held the traditional rice and raisin pudding, surmounted by mounds of cookies of all shapes and colors.

Unfortunately, access to the pudding and the ribs were strictly bound by tradition. It required that one begin with the lutefisk. The young people were all seated at a separate long table. A yellow, quivering gelatinous mass was plopped down in each of our plates. The adults stood smiling in the background as they observed the drama unfold. I had found that inhaling just as I took the obligatory bite considerably reduced the pain of the moment. There was a perfunctory clapping as each young hero earned the right to call themselves a real Norwegian.

The dining room was dominated by two long tables and, standing in the corner, a huge Christmas tree. With all due credit to Grandpa, their tree always looked as close to perfect as could be expected of a tree growing in wild. Mike and I observed their trees through the eyes of true connoisseurs. But our attention was riveted to the avalanche of boxes, cylinders, flat pieces, and bundles all done up in paper of different colors. Each year the family agreed that they would draw names so that each person bought only one present. But then each family would throw in an extra three or four presents to be exchanged within a household, plus a few odds and ends. As a result each sleigh always arrived totally full. The gifting always managed to be out of control, so each sleigh generally returned equally full as well.

By the time the raisin pudding, as well as the Yule Kakka, and the cookies appeared, you could already hear the sounds of dishes being done. Each year there was the announcement: "First the dishes, then the presents." The younger set viewed this as yet another example of how Norwegian values and standards were taught. Each year also produced the decision among the adults that instead of a group orgy of ripping paper and rending boxes, we would follow a more controlled, sedate process. One of the older children would walk to the tree and pick up a present at random and then read the tag. Then they would then deliver the present to the recipient. Thirty pairs of eyes would center on the labored process of removing the wrapping; some even folded it, much to the consternation of the younger set. There would also be an appropriate comment or two from the giver. This was the plan. Each year it would begin, just so. Grandma and the aunts would sit beaming and nodding their heads. But by the fifth present or so, the process would began to fray. The momentum would pick up and slip into serious disarray as two or three additional children would slip into the ritual. The process would speed up such that the thank-you speeches were short-circuited, and two or three names were being read at the same time. Finally, there was no one listening and things would build to a natural crescendo of laughing, shredding, exclamation, and ripping boxes from their wrappings in an un-seemly fashion. With the last present had been opened, an ex-hausted silence would follow. The dining room floor would be covered with gift boxes, ribbons, and paper. Grandma sitting in her rocker smiling and saying goodnight as one family after an-other slipped out the door to fill the sleighs for the trip home. We all understood Grandma's wish to make the evening last longer. But like the rest of the children, she was herself incapable of hold-ing a joyful moment back. She had to ride the crest of the moment and just go with it—Yule Kakka, tree, presents, lutefisk, and all.

3

The Novice

In a community such as Robinson Lake, thirteen- and four-teen-year-old boys are an indispensable commodity. Growing up, we became useful additions to many adult activities. Being big enough to carry a pack would get you an invitation to come along for spring beaver trapping. Then, during the summer, you'd be asked to help trap minnows. This involved emptying traps in the minnow swamp into buckets, which we'd hang on a carved wooden yolk as we made our way from the swamp to the boat a half-mile away. These were day-long expeditions.

By age fifteen and sixteen, it was time to begin serious em-ployment. Each of us would go to Uncle Hank, who was the fore-man of the track gang at Robinson Lake. He and several of my uncles rode the speeder every day to check the rails. In spring they would add extra men and continue the perpetual battle to keep the roadbed from sinking into the muskeg. Our job was to replace the oak ties that had rotted out. Sometimes we also laid steel for spur lines on new roadbeds. The day would begin riding out in the early morning on the speeder, going forty miles an hour, into a new day. The berry picking places would flash by, as would the creek where the northern pike came out of Armstrong Lake, the black cliffs by Fourth Lake Eagle Nest where Dad got a deer, and the spruce swamp where Jenny and Hugo lived. Then we "men" would lift the speeder off the rails to a siding and drink our first cup of coffee while Hank made his fateful walk up the track. Inevitably, he would then spot where the ties rails sagged several inches, though you could usually only see it by putting your face on the track. "All right, boys, let's raise 'er up a little," he'd say. Then it would begin—the process of jacking up the rails and ties and then forcing gravel under the ties with a shovel. Each day was slightly different. But after a few weeks scything grass, smoothing road beds, raising tracks, cutting brush, and laying steel, it would all blend together into a comfortable pattern.

This was a course followed by all of my brothers and cousins, it was a kind of family trajectory that was understood and valued. Our traditions contained a set of subtle but gentle constraints that kept each of us moving in a similar direction. There was the certainty of a fixed amount of money. Everyone understood who you were and what you were doing. Then there was the flat certainty that every day would be like every other. If you accepted the virtues of the path, you could be comfortable for life knowing that you had found your place in the sun. In my case, adolescence brought with it changes that eventually led me to a new path away from Robinson Lake.

It began with a chance encounter at school that deflected me ever so slightly from the family's path. In the spring, the school had announced a birding contest. At that time of year, Robinson Lake was a part of a major annual bird migration. A huge variety of birds loved the swamps in our lake basin. I bought a bird book and began making my list. Each day of the contest, I appeared at the top or close to the top of the list, but there was one name that kept appearing above or right next to mine: Robert Olson. Eventually, we met. I don't remember who actually won the contest, but the event set the occasion for a friendship that has lasted several decades. Bob was smaller than most of us, but well set up. There was a sort of a lean racer quality to the way that he moved. He was very quick and easy to laugh. By the time we entered high school we had become close friends, and spent a good deal of time together exploring algebra, girls, and the other great mysteries. In the spring of our sophomore year, he called the section house to say that his father had heard that they were opening a Boy Scout regional canoe base up on Fernberg Road at Moose Lake. They wanted swampers to work with their canoe guides, taking Scout groups up into the boundary waters. It seemed unlikely that we would earn very much, but we might be able to spend a lot of time in the wilderness area up on the Canadian Border.

We drove to Moose Lake and eventually arrived at the newly constructed log outbuildings of the outfitting base. Hod Ludlow, the manager, was tall and slightly stooped, without an ounce of fat anywhere that I could see. He had big hands and there was a lot of eye contact as we talked. His laugh was infectious. There were no formal agreements, no contracts to sign. The nature of the tasks to be performed was left unspecified. Bob and I were the only locals at the base, although the program was jammed with young men only slightly older than we from all over the country.

Our initial task was to get the base ready for the first groups of scouts who would arrive in the next two weeks. Everything smelled new and fresh, the logs forming the main lodge and warehouse had not even been stained. The area outside the lodge was littered with logs, wood chips, and piles of gravel. Inside, there was a virtual symphony of odors, ranging from the smell of linseed oil in one corner to varnish, wood stain, and new canvas tarps in another. In the warehouse, the staff constructed bins for dehydrated fruit, milk, and potatoes, counters for packs, tents, ground cloths, axes, and army blankets.

Each of the staff went through practice sessions in canoeing, packing, first aid, and plant identification. Those of us unfamiliar with scouting were sent off to Wisconsin for a week's course at the Waterfront Director School. I was entirely innocent of any scouting experience, so was sent off a week prior to the base opening. For the first time, I learned about the technology of paddling a canoe, J-strokes, bow rudders, and sweeps. A tiny man with a huge voice, appropriately named The Major, pushed us from dawn to dark. We learned how to empty a canoe full of water, whether you were in the water yourself or in another canoe. Admission to the mess hall required that first you observe the knot the Major tied as he stood in the doorway, and then reproduce it yourself. I was always last to get into the hall. Classes in lifesaving were interspersed with classes in waterfront safety, rowing, and swimming. It was not enough to be able to paddle a canoe; it was also necessary to learn to propel it without a paddle. To do this, you stand on the gunwale behind the stern seat and pump with your legs. It is still a great trick. If you also paddle while you pump, you can get an astonishing rate of speed going in a short period of time. My addition of a paddle was strictly playful and therefore was not a part of The Major's manual.

By late early summer, I had become a full-fledged swamper. Sporting brand new Jefferson logger boots with the long laces tied in a square knot in the back, so that six inches of lace hung down. Fringed dew flaps were laced to hold across the toe. The long knife was worn next to a bright handkerchief which hung like a sash from the belt on the right side. The handkerchief was used as headband, pot-holder, or bandage, but its main function was to add color and movement when you walked. Each of us added festoons of rope, string, and leather to the belt, which enhanced the whole effect. It was a special treat to drive into Ely for supplies. With our long hair, red sashes, strings flying, and huge boots freshly greased, we were forerunners for the 1960 hippie costume. The eighteenth-century voyageurs had dressed in the same exuberant style and probably for very much the same reason. The clothing and equipment were statements about what is functional in the bush and what is not. It is only in the city that it seems like a costume, because it is.

The Scout base reflected an attitude toward the wilderness that was very different from the Robinson Lake perspective. For the family, going into the woods was as functional as going shopping in Ely. You went to the city for a purpose. In the same vein, when we went into the woods it was for a clear purpose: to get wood, to get fish, to lay in meat, or to put up ice. Sometimes it was beautiful, and sometimes it was frightening. You enjoyed being a part of it all but it did not involve you in any sense of mission. The Scout base was different. It communicated the idea of a greater purpose than just catching a fish. There was a real sense of excitement to learning that you could become part of a mission, led by individuals who were real heroes. Fulfilling the mission required that you steadily acquire an enormous range of skills and be able to practice them at a very high level. Some of the adults who talked to us about this larger mission had the characteristics of a Zen master. They had incredible knowledge about nature and a very high order of skills as outdoorsmen.

As swampers we were about as articulate about this mission as young salmon moving upstream. The formula was something like Speed + Distance = Success as a voyageur. Whoever could cover the greatest distance in a day or a week was obviously a high status person. The Scouts were assigned three to a canoe, so that portages could be covered in one trip. Three paddlers instead of two meant that impossible distances could be paddled in a single day. We cruised to the edge of the map, paddling from dawn till dark and sometimes traveling after dark as well. Each return to the base brought news of lakes and rivers from the far edge of the map. Going from Mack Lake to the east of Kwanipi required following the twenty miles of the Wawiag River to the edge of the Quetico map. Alternatively, a party of Scouts traveling at their normal speed could get to Pickerel Narrows at the northern edge in four or five days. Three paddlers traveling very light could perhaps do it in one or two days.

Living at the Scout base with several dozen boy-men was like being in an area frequented by summer rain-squalls. Things would be calm and peaceful, then suddenly there would be a lightning burst of excitement: The wind is howling down Moose Lake tonight, pushing waves two and three feet high. Let's paddle to

Basswood Lake! Let's go, just us three guys! There was nothing like being out in the black water, wind, and rain, three boy-men laughing, howling at the sheer joy of riding the canoe over waves that lifted and surged like horses. We'd hit Newfound Lake and Sucker before dawn, then roll up in sleeping bags on the first big island in Basswood Lake.

Given the emphasis upon speed, the base allotted little time for fishing. Unless we were short of food, fishing was time taken away from traveling, and therefore time wasted. However, one particular ten day trip to Kashipiwi and down Sturgeon Lake to Phoobah Lake ended up being a notable exception. By the fourth day, the guide knew he had misjudged. We were short of food. We were deep into the Quetico and no one was willing to turn back or shorten the trip. As a result the end of each day, fishing became a very important activity. We consumed enormous amounts of filleted walleye and northern pike, yet still, there was simply not enough food. The guide decided that the swamper and two stalwarts would take a sixteen-foot Old Town canoe and cut across at Miner Lake to M'Acree, Crooked, Basswood, and back to Moose Lake. There we would load up a hundred pounds of supplies and retrace our route to catch up with the party.

The magnificent three were given extra rations of peanut butter and hardtack as fuel for the "mission." Our one pack contained sleeping bags, rain gear, and a tent. As we left, we passed the group standing along the burnt-out shoreline eating their breakfast of cornmeal mush, fish, and dehydrated fruit. We stormed off under full peanut butter power. Fully conscious of our mission, we raced fourteen hours a day back to the canoe base at Moose Lake where we were treated with utmost deference as men of grave purpose. Would we rest the night there? No indeed; our comrades awaited us somewhere north of the Crooked River. As we pushed through Newfound and Sucker Lakes, the wind rose steadily. We made good time across the first protected bay in Basswood Lake. Ahead we could see the huge rollers coming in from Bailey Bay.

We rounded the corner at mid-afternoon to face a wind from the west. It had a full ten-mile sweep. Magnificent black combers rolled across the bay right into us. We slipped briefly into the lee side of an island conveniently placed in the neck of the channel leading out to the full fury of the bay. We had a hero's feast of chocolate, hardtack, and peanut butter. A sixteen foot canoe with 450 pounds of fringed, beaded muscle has very little freeboard. Throwing in 100 pounds of rations, three pairs of heavy boots, and an equipment pack put the operation in real jeopardy. None of us had ever paddled in waves of the size we encountered. However, there was never any doubt in our minds that we would prevail.

Our only concession to the wind and waves was to remove the boots and tie them to the thwarts. We backed into the lee for sixty feet or so to give ourselves a running start on the situation. The three of us straining at the paddles lifted the bow out of the water with each synchronous stroke added to our growing sense of invincibility. We cleared the point by a good sixty feet before encountering the full force of the wind. The first comber rose gracefully under us as we powered into it. The front half of the canoe slid endlessly up into the sky. The bowman's paddle could not reach the water. When we slammed down into the trough, he was thrown out of his seat, but managed to stay in the canoe. The remaining two paddlers kept up the stroke and drove into the huge mass of water rolling in behind it. The tiny canoe cut through the top of it, but the wave continued to swell and dump in bathtubs of water over the sides of the canoe. The next two waves filled the canoe to the gunwales. The canoe had become so unstable that all three of us were forced to sit on the bottom. We sat in stunned silence as the waves roared past us, our boots floating about in the canoe.

There are some things that are just bigger than life. The combers in Bailey Bay were a case in point. This was just the first of many episodes where we learned that spirit and unlimited energy are not always sufficient by themselves. We paddled backwards with our hands until the wind deposited us once again in the lee of the island. We landed, made soup, dried out, and waited for the wind to die down with a newfound respect. We eventually caught up with our fish-eating colleagues and were accorded proper heroes welcomes.

The end of summer marked a ninety-day introduction to the bush. I had traveled through most of the major routes in the boundary waters and Quetico. I could say that I "knew" the details of three or four of the standard routes, such as the Agnes, Silence Lake chain, the Kashipiwi and Kwanipi loop, or the Sarah to McIntyre to Side Lake trip. I knew a little about camp cooking, how to find portages, and how to read maps. I knew a lot about paddling and how to rig a mast to run before the wind. I returned to Robinson Lake in September badly in need of a haircut, with tattered boots, shredded clothes, a long sharp knife, and ninety-seven dollars in cash. The family was shocked and pointed out that I could have made that much money in two weeks on the track gang.

At first, people listened politely to my accounts of trips to lakes with unknown names, then it was time to make wood, put up the ice, and hunt deer. Everything quickly went back to the way it had always been. But for me, a new piece had been added to the pattern. I was no longer content with life on the edge of the bush. I had met young men from all over the country, and I wanted to experience some of what they described. I thought I should become part of the mission to protect wilderness rather than just take from it. I wanted to continue growing in outdoor skills. I had met adults that summer who had many of these components, so I knew it could be done. I wanted to find new paths rather than endlessly repeat the familiar loops. Over time, this slight deflection from the family's path was like the first tentative finger reaching out from the riverbed, just before the spring flood arrives and cuts a new course.

4

The Apprentice

The next spring, I contacted Hod Ludlow and he wrote back saying I could be a full-fledged guide for the Scout base the following summer. World War II was beginning; at this point it was just a distant flicker of newsreels and headlines, but not directly a part of our world. However, numbers of young men from Ely had already been drafted, including a half dozen canoe guides who worked for the Border Lakes and Wilderness Outfitters.

Both Bob and I had planned to spend a second year at the Scout base. It was still late May and we were spending the weekend painting the outside of his father's warehouse at Border Lakes Outfitters. The warehouse was situated outside of Winton on the west end of Fall Lake. Winton had fallen from grace since its glory days as a sawmill town. Main Street consisted of only a few graying stores and one or two weather-beaten taverns. The only buildings that had known paint in recent times were the railroad station and the Outfitting warehouse.

Border Lake Outfitters was ideally situated on Fall Lake, which, in turn, was connected by a four mile truck portage to Basswood Lake. Basswood was the magic portal to one of the world's few international wilderness areas. On the U.S. side there was the Boundary Waters, and on the Canadian side the Quetico. No one really knows how many lakes are contained in these two areas, but together their boundaries define world-class wilderness cruising by canoe. You could start paddling from the Border Lakes Outfitters and be in Basswood Lake by the first day. From there you could go east to Lake Superior or northwest to Lake Athabasca and Hudson's Bay. Historically Basswood Lake was pivotal to wilderness travel. At one point it even had its own Hudson's Bay post.

The warehouse presided over the west end of Fall Lake. Two stories high, the tents and canvas tarps were kept up on the top floor. The supplies, packing area, and office were on the first floor. The long roofline sagged gently at its middle, the walls were tilted slightly toward the east. Everything functioned properly, but there were braces and patches everywhere. The building spoke to the fact that Bob's father Sig had started the first outfitting company in Ely almost a quarter of a century ago. He was also one of the first canoe guides in that area. Over the years Sig had slowly built up a cadre of professional guides, such as John Sengstead, Hollis Latterell, and Francis Santineau. Sig's oldest son, Sig Junior, had also become part of this elite group.

Each spring the warehouse was patched, braced, and painted on the outside. The inside was left to nature. The wood by now had aged to deep rich colors that could not come from a can or brush. As the spring morning heated up, the tents hanging from the ceiling gave off an aroma as thick and distinctive as freshly baked bread. Several of the guides were working upstairs sanding and painting some of the sixty-five wood and canvas canoes. Broken ribs were patched and tears in the canvas mended. The patching and repairing marked the beginning of each season. For weeks prior to the first trip going out, the warehouse was given over to the rich smell of the glue, resin, and paint overlaid with the odor of tents baking in the loft.

There was a deep sense of order, at the Border Lake Warehouse, here with none of the explosive electricity that had characterized the Scout base. Here the guides did not dress in any way that would mark them as distinct. Sengstead stood a very compact five foot ten inches, and usually dressed in clean Levis, blue work shirts, and boots. There was nothing about him in particular that said "guide," but there was an air of quiet competence that made you listen when he talked.

Bob and I were painting outside under the big door in the loft. It was opened when canoes were passed in or out of the warehouse. Sengstead was working up in the loft on several old Thompson model 16-footers upended on sawhorses. Two of his buddies were sitting on stacks of equipment. The low murmur of their voices drifted down in the morning air. Bob's father, Sig came out of the office door, inspected the new color, smiled approvingly, and said, "Pat, would you come to my office for a minute?" We walked through the store with its racks of maps and glass cases of fishing and camping gear. The floor gently sloped from the middle to each wall. As we sat down, he started to light one of the many pipes lying on his desk. "Were you planning on guiding for the Scout base this summer?" I replied, "Yes, I think so. Hod Ludlow said we were invited back." It was hard to keep a touch of pride from my voice. He looked at me carefully and said, "What would you think of also taking out trips for Border Lakes this summer? I have two trips right now that I think you could handle very well." I'm sure my face registered simultaneous shock and pleasure. I barely succeeded in nodding my head. I had not thought of myself as being anywhere near ready to becoming a professional. The top half of his face was visible over the two hands still lighting his pipe. He was smiling, and said, "Ah, does that mean yes?"

"Yes. Thanks! I would like . . . Who are they?" I struggled with a strange mix of panic and pleasure. Images of what could go wrong stampeded through my mind, but at the same time I felt a tremendous sense of honor to have been asked. I couldn't stay focused. I was glad that Sig continued so I was not required to talk much. He went on to explain the first trip would be for an experienced party named Strauss. Mr. Strauss would arrive in Winton on June 12th. He had been to the Quetico several times. All he and his group required was a swamper to assist with the portaging and the

61

cooking. I would, however, receive a regular guide's wages. Because several of the guides were being drafted, both Bob and I would begin our apprenticeships this summer. We would also be working as swampers for experienced guides whenever possible. Some of the easy ones, like the Strauss trip, we would be taking out by ourselves.

It turned out that Strauss had not only been to the Quetico before, but also knew exactly where he wanted to go: Agnes Lake. As he said in his letter, he would bring two friends in for a five day fishing trip. His letter was brief and businesslike. In his prior trips, he had been with Joe Chosa. He was sorry that Joe was not available for that week. I wished I were taking out someone less experienced.

All of the equipment was selected with great care and then double-checked. There was a four-man wall tent with a floor and mosquito bar for the party to sleep in. The guide slept by himself in a two-man tent, also with floor and mosquito bar. Both of these were carefully folded and served as backing for the kettle pack. Next came the cloth sack enclosing the cooking grate; then the sack with the nested cooking pots, plates, and utensils. A lightweight camp axe, first aid kit, and the 8 x 10 foot rain tarp on top completed that load. Two heavy wool blankets for each person served as backing for the long line of food packs. All of the food was removed from packages or crates and packed in linen bags, each with a drawstring at the top. Each bag was labeled for its contents, but it was seldom that these labels were necessary. Fingertips groping in the bottom of the Duluth pack soon learned to translate texture and weight. Anything could be found within a few minutes because the food was packed separately by meals. Depending upon the length of the trip, there were one or two breakfast packs. One dinner pack would have cans (this was 1943), and the other fresh vegetables and ham to be eaten in the first few days.

The lunch pack was constructed from cardboard boxes cut to

fit within a # 4 Duluth pack. The lunch pack was often a work of art, because its multifaceted functions were so important to the well-being of the party. Fresh bread was packed in it in such a way that it would not be crushed even when it was thrown on top of a heavier pack for portaging. What made this a particularly delicate operation was that several dozen eggs formed the core of this pack. The cartons of eggs were rolled in cardboard and taped, and then each cylinder was inserted inside its own surrounding wall of bread. There were also jars of jam rolled in cardboard cylinders to be inserted along the sides. The bread would survive for five days or more if we got good weather; longer trips were fueled by hard-tack. Trips longer than two weeks required the baking of bannock. Usually the lunch pack was given to the most sure-of-foot, the packer who never falls, and the packer who never flips the top pack to the ground but gently lowers it. Even so, on most trips the casualty rate for eggs was high; the crisis, usually gave itself away by the unmistakable odor of rotting eggs.

I tried not to think of all the things that could go wrong. Going over the packs twice helped. That morning Sig had talked to me for about an hour. I mainly listened. He began by gently suggesting that the objective be comfort rather than speed. Many of the parties would consist of older men who could not be expected to double pack or even to make two trips on the portage. The second, third, and fourth trips across the portage would be my responsibility. Members of the party often carry only their own personal pack and fishing gear. Although occasionally one of them might carry a canoe or a lighter equipment pack, this would not happen very often. In other words, the plan should be for a slow-paced journey to a base camp and a serious focus upon fishing.

Sig's last bit of advice was given with such emphasis that the details stand out six decades later. He was staring out the window as if he were visualizing what he was telling me, motioning with the pipe as he talked, "Don't worry about the cooking; you'll do fine on that. It is not so much what you give them as how you do it." He dropped his chin down to his chest and looked at me intently. "Make it an occasion; make it enjoyable. Spread a poncho and set the table." I looked surprised. "No, that's right, Pat. No matter what, set a table. Put the dishes and utensils around, salt and pepper, everything they will need. Once they sit down, everything is where they can reach it. And one more thing: if you can find some flowers, put them in the center." I sat in stunned silence and just nodded my head. Good God, flowers! Now, years later, starting on my second thousand days in the bush, I understand why he gave me this advice. Even now, my final act in preparing dinner is often to split a green alder stick, insert a flower in its cleft, and carefully place it as a centerpiece. Each time the ritual is repeated, I remember Sig.

Mr. Strauss, the writer of the terse businesslike letter, was to arrive in ten minutes. I stood on the platform of the train station at Winton, Minnesota, with a deep sense of dread. When I awakened that morning, I had even thought of calling and saying I was sick. I did not mention this to my mother as she gave me my bundle of fresh clothes and a loaf of brown bread. I said nothing about my fear as my father drove me into town. I heard the speeder start up and move off down the tracks with Hank and his crew. I fervently wished I could be there with them.

There was a ring of 1930s vintage Dodge and Ford trucks parked close to the train platform. Each of them was rigged like the one I had driven in from Border Lakes. A flatbed in back was ringed with benches; the roof and sides had loops and straps for tying off canoes. Such a truck could carry a dozen tourists, their baggage, and a half-dozen canoes. Each truck was marked by a panel on the side identifying one of the two canoe-outfitting companies or some nationally known fishing camp on Basswood Lake. There were a number of tourists waiting to catch the train, some of them returning from a week or more in the bush. Even though their faces were brown and they wore similar clothes and equipment, they did not quite look like the guides. I had a beaten-up bush hat, a new pair of Jefferson logger boots without caulks, a new black and white wool shirt, and a pair of waterproof canvas pants washed three times so they would not look too new. There were no fringes or sash, but the bootlaces were again tied off in back.

I talked to Hollis as we waited. He stood over six feet tall, almost too tall for a canoe guide. He had jet-black hair and mustache and he was always laughing, always moving and talking with his hands. He was the focal point of the platform: He looked like a canoe guide. Like many of the other guides, Hollis trapped in the winter and guided in the summertime. He was telling stories about that spring's beaver trapping, but I could hardly listen. Then, in mid-sentence, Hollis turned, stared down the tracks, and said, "There she comes. I can hear it. Well, Jer, I'll look for you around Burke Lake. Maybe have supper together there. Catch nothing but big ones." He gave me a big grin as he set the brim of the World War I campaign hat square to his face and stood back in his boots.

As the Duluth, Misabe, and Iron Range Special steamed to a halt, the flood of tourists, fishing rods, cameras, wool shirts, and packs poured from the train. A burly, middle-aged man with a case of rods asked Hollis for Border Lakes. Hollis jerked his thumb toward me. I introduced myself to Mr. Strauss. His face reflected no surprise. He told me later that he thought I was older than sixteen, and if he had known he would have been upset. His companions seemed about the same age as Strauss, and like him, they seemed a little too heavy for a canoe. They were excited to be starting and hardly noticed me. It was a relief to be caught up in the details of loading the truck and driving off to the Outfitters.

Bob's father was standing at the door in front of Border Lakes as we drove up. His uniform for all seasons was ultra clean and well-worn: army suntans with thick wool socks, moccasins, and a pipe. He and Mr. Strauss greeted each other as old friends. Within an hour our gear was loaded on the trolley and being lowered down the tracks to the dock on Fall Lake, where Peterson's launch was waiting. We had already walked down the dirt road to the tiny U.S. Customs office. Strauss had systematically worked his way through the case of spoons and plugs at the warehouse, adding to his already impressive collection. I was pleased to notice that when he asked for my suggestions he actually listened to what I had to say. We added to his supply of KB spoons and lead weights because I expected that we would lose a great many on our trip.

The packs were loaded in back of the launch, then the driver, Bud Larsen, and I tied the towrope through the front seat to loop under the bow of the first canoe. From that we drew a line from the first canoe to the second, as Bud put the launch in gear and pulled away from the dock, I held the towline. Under full speed, the first canoe was tied off so its bow rode up high on the crest of the third standing wave. We made no stops going up Fall Lake to the four-mile truck portage into Basswood.

The routines of filing through customs, packing the launch, and setting up for the tow were familiar; but being a guide and responsible for adults four times my age was completely new. I did not know just how to proceed. I went to the rear of the launch and checked the packs to be sure that there were nine of them, and that each was tagged "Strauss." I finally sat down next to the group. Strauss had been through all of this several times. He was going on at some length about his earlier trips. He even knew where we would camp that evening. I sat and listened for a moment. Not knowing what else to do, I reached in my pocket for the carborundum stone and I began to sharpen the sheath knife I carried. It was already razor sharp, but I worked away at it as the animated conversation flowed around me. At Robinson Lake, a knife is not sharp unless it can be used to skin a beaver or cut up a deer. The proper test is to cut hair. As I listened to the men talk, I casually rolled up my pant leg and wet a hairy patch of my leg. The conversation slowed as I shaved off three square inches of hair. Knives appeared as if by magic, and suddenly I was included in the conversation too.

66

The trip was a great success. Early in the spring, the big Northern were still in the south end of Agnes Lake. The trout fishing in Lake Louise was spectacular. Lake Agnes is like a hub with trip routes spreading from it in all directions. My party became expert in getting fishing data from passing groups and by the second or third day they could see that they were catching more than their share. The day before our return, the group decided that they could take an afternoon off and go for a bath at Louise Falls. The portage trail into Lake Louise starts up a steep hill that climbs along a raging torrent. Halfway up, there is a tiny pool that can hold three people comfortably. You can sit in the pool with your back to a cliff, which is sort of like being on a balcony overlooking the south end of the lake. The water drops straight down the cliff for about thirty feet, which feels like a shower with the water turned on full blast. The three of them sat in the tub not saying much, but you could see that they felt they had really done it. I brought up the lunch pack and put all of the dainties we had left on the poncho. I couldn't find a flower, but it was not needed.

When we returned to Border Lakes, Mr. Strauss sang my praises to Sig, saying that I was a perfect companion. He also mentioned in passing, "That there were even flowers on the dinner table." He would return again, first with his two brothers and later still with his son.

There were no trips scheduled for the next three weeks, so I was sent to Peterson's fishing camp on Basswood. I was to be an assistant lake guide to Joe Chosa, he had a party coming in that would require two boats. My job would be simple: just follow him around, stay out of his way, and keep the people happy. When we met, he simply nodded his head in my direction and then at some point stared off to the side. It made me uncomfortable, but didn't call for me to do anything in particular. My impulse had been to mention that I had taken one of his old parties out for a five day trip. It was very clear, however, that this was not the time.

I had met the Peterson launch at the public dock in Winton. It was loaded with a dozen tourists. They all squeezed, as best they could, into the cabin that ran about half the length of the boat. Crates of food, boxes of liquor, and piles of suitcases filled the back of the boat. Pete, the owner, was driving the launch himself that day. Pete was a close friend of the Olsons, so we had met before. As a boy, I had also worked for him at his fishing camp on Basswood Lake.

Pete was one of those tall, thin people, perpetually hunched over as if the ceiling was never quite high enough. Winter, summer, and fall, he wore a faded brown duck hunter's hat. He didn't smile much, but his habit of squinting gave his face a very thoughtful cast. His normal expression conveyed a borderline sense of disapproval. Owning and running a fishing camp meant that something was forever out of kilter. There was always a motor that wouldn't start, a water line that didn't work, a party of four that didn't appear at the train station, or just plain bad weather. The man had a lot to worry about. I stood up front beside him as he squinted through the rain driving against the windshield. The waves were building quickly into solid black masses, moving in line against the boat. He was concentrating intensely on controlling his speed, quartering into the waves and tacking first to one quarter, then the other.

The tourists sat on the benches in the back of the truck. We loaded the boxes and crates around their feet, and then fastened the rain tarps down on the sides. I sat up front in his old truck as it labored around the potholes that decorated the Chosa tote road. The road accommodated itself to the terrain. It went around glaciated rock ridges, not through them. It skirted swamps and one small lake. We began talking quietly, first about the weather, then about the party waiting for me at the lodge. Pete hardly noticed the potholes in the road as he zeroed in on his analysis of modern times and the forces that brought us to World War II. Midway across he launched into his favorite topic, technocracy and Bellamy's *Looking Backward from the Year Two Thousand*. Pete, like many intelligent people living in transition country, was self-taught, but he held deeply felt philosophical convictions. His quiet voice was barely audible over the roar of the engine as he downshifted for the next hill. "We can have a better world, dammit. Better technology and a more logical basis for deciding things." His big hands gripped the steering wheel as he shook his head and glared at the road. "We could make it happen. We know how to feed everybody. We know how to put a roof over people's heads." We were to have this conversation many times. Buying Bellamy's book was the first of many that I bought at his behest. He was looking for champions; I didn't know it, but I was beginning to look for causes. Pete, Sig, and some of the adults at the Scout base represented to me a new kind of adult committed to a mission outside of self.

The party I was to work with was a Mr. Ross and a friend. Both were bulldog fishermen; the problem was that their wives were not. Basswood Lake in the 1940s offered some of the best walleye and Northern fishing in the world. Within a day's travel by canoe, there was also first class bass and lake trout fishing. There were three or four fishing camps on the lake. With their outside privies and wood stoves, each cabin was comfortable, but Spartan. The amenities were pared down to what a fisherman would settle for if he were catching world-class fish. Wives and families posed a special problem.

The resort staff and the lake guides filed into the kitchen at five in the morning to sit at a long wooden table. Josie and her crew had been up for an hour packing the wooden food boxes for the boats that would spend all day on the lake. Each box contained its own small but complete kitchen with everything needed to cook a fish luncheon. They were ready to feed the staff bacon, eggs, potatoes, oatmeal, and pancakes in any combination and in any quantity. People came in and sat down quietly. There was some very gentle joshing, mainly with Josie the cook. There were a half dozen lake guides there, all giving breakfast serious attention. As he finished eating, one of the guides looked up. "So Tony, which part of the lake you going to fish today?" Tony and Joe Chosa, his brother, were sitting together at the end of the table. Neither of them looked up, nor did they stop eating. The two of them were the central figures at the table every morning and evening that they worked at Pete's. The younger brother, Tony, was the best fishermen on the lake. He was called Two Ton Tony. Legend had it that every year, for as long as anyone could remember, he and the tourists in his boat caught over 4000 pounds of fish. After a long pause, Tony simply said, "Darkfish Bay." He didn't bother to look at his questioner. All other guides feigned indifference as if they were not listening to the exchange yet. All other conversation had stopped when Tony made his reply.

This was the beginning of the daily ritual. Tony and his brother Joe had the best motors in Pete's fishing camp. Both of them had fine-tuned the old Lockwood 10-horse engines used at Pete's to get maximum speed. In fact they were noticeably faster, so that on a long five-mile reach they could pull away from the pack of boats following at a discreet distance. They would slip behind any one of a dozen islands, drop anchor, and begin fishing immediately. Sometimes the spot was a dummy, and they would stay only long enough for the other boats to spot them and move in. The other guides might work at such a dry hole for several days while Tony or Joe were off fishing a reef in a back bay that had been known to their family for years. Basswood Lake was the Chosa family's playground. The rest of us only worked there.

Lake guiding brought me little joy. It was a pleasure to walk down the dock to a waiting boat that you had carefully cleaned and loaded, and I liked cutting a line through the narrows to the big water to the east, with all of us rested and sensing the morning. But being there also meant I was at the mercy of a greasy, noisy outboard engine, the sounds and smells of which set you apart from the bush itself. I was basically in the company of people who were keeping score on themselves, on me, and on everyone else. The day was defined by the number and size of fish caught.

Joe had little choice but to allow me to share some of his knowledge of fishing holes. However, there were some things that he did not share. Our two boats might begin trolling together when suddenly Joe would disappear around the corner. An hour or two later, he would reappear with a half dozen walleyes. The guide who caught the most fish spent the most days on the lake. Guides who did not produce fish were sent home in disgrace. There never was any doubt about who was number one. At the end of the day the camp staff, guests, and guides not in service sat on benches at the end of the dock. Each guide followed his party off the dock carrying that day's catch for all to see and evaluate.

There was never anything remarkable about my catches for the eight days with the Ross party, but being allowed to follow Joe made it possible to make a creditable showing. Gradually it fell to me to take the two wives fishing. Mr. Ross explained the arrangement to me early one morning on the dock. Joe stood there watching my face, but saying nothing. Joe was slightly balding, his skin a deep color, with wide cheekbones and a flattened nose. He seldom spoke and never engaged in small talk. In the days and weeks that we spent together, I'm not sure we exchanged more than a few hundred words. Listening to Mr. Ross's instruction, I'm sure he was glad to be relieved of the burden of a second boat tailing him. I also knew that having people in his boat that did not care for fishing meant to him that he would come off the lake early with a shorter string of fish.

Without a backward glance, Joe roared away from the dock loaded with the two bulldog fishermen. I was left standing on the dock with two ladies in flowered hats. I decided to start at the beginning and see if I could gently nudge either of them into fishing. We went up into Back Bay a short distance away. It was relatively shallow there with a good collection of weeds and lily pads. The two of them trolled large plugs. There were no walleyes in that particular area, but there was an unlimited supply of small Northern pike. The fish seemed to be hitting anything that moved and kept the boat in a beehive of activity. I was never able to row very far before one of them would shout, "Fish!" I explained that if one of them had a fish, the other was to take in their line, but in the excitement of the chase they seldom remembered to do this. This was not part of a contest. All of us were having a great time. I was very busy with my pliers removing plugs from thoroughly irritated Northerns. The ladies did agree that it was all right for me to throw the small four and five pounders back as "practice" fish.

We moved slowly through the morning and took an extra half hour for lunch. The lake was hot now, and very still. No one seemed in a hurry as we returned to the boat. As we rowed along a green wall of snake grass, Mrs. Ross sat up in the bow facing the shore as she made short, workmanlike casts with her red and white surface plug. There was a splash, then a shout. "Pat, what should I do?" I stood up and saw a shark-like shadow moving at great speed across the shallow mud flats. Mrs. Ross stood frozen with both hands gripping the reel. The rod bent at a sharp angle with its tip pointing fingerlike at the great Northern pike now thrashing about. Before I could say anything, he had snapped the 10 pound test line and streaked off into deeper water.

All three of us were electrified by the event. There was much excited talking as I went over the steps of setting a hook and then getting the fish on the braking system built into their reels. After a brief practice we had two casters in the boat instead of one. Mrs. Ross kept firm control over the bow and began telling me which sections of shoreline she wished to work next. She was no longer just a passenger; she was fishing. We began to accumulate a very interesting stringer of Northern pike, each well over five pounds and over thirty inches long.

The women ended up as the heroes of that evening's dockside ritual. Mrs. Ross's story of the great beast of Back Bay was told and retold several times that evening. In the days that followed, she convinced her husband that even if walleyes were "better," Northerns were a lot more fun, especially if you caught them casting. When they left at the end of the week, Joe and I each received a check and a handshake from Mr. Ross. Pete was down at the dock too as the launch took the party to Four Mile Portage and the trip back to Ely. "They looked pretty happy, Jerry," he told me. "You must have done something right. What you get for a tip?" I showed him the hundred-dollar bill clipped to the check. "Jesus!" he exclaimed and shot me a rare smile. "That's as much as Joe got. He isn't going to like that much." He touched my shoulder as he turned and walked off the dock. I was surprised and elated. I felt as if I had climbed over a huge hurdle.

When I came in from my next canoe trip, there was a note from Pete saying that he had another party coming. They had hired Joe Chosa. They would base at Pete's fishing camp and take a series of short canoe trips out of North Bay. Could I come and serve again as Joe's swamper for a few days? This was the first time anyone had asked for me specifically. I was very excited, but tried to be very cool as I explained to my mother that I needed clean clothes that same day. I added, "I need to catch a floatplane for Basswood Lake later this afternoon." I felt very professional as I carried my personal pack up the road at Robinson to catch the train for Ely, in worn but clean canvas pants, cut high to reveal wool socks, tightly laced Jefferson logger boots, a black and white checked wool shirt, a bush hat, and a Duluth pack full of gear. I felt like I stood apart from the tourists sitting on the same train. The pilot met me at the dock on Shagawa Lake just outside Ely.

We loaded the fresh meat Pete had ordered and a few other boxes, and then taxied out into the lake. As the pilot accelerated, the cabin filled with the engine sound. The plane rocked back slightly on its pontoons and quickly moved to speeds far beyond anything I had experienced on a lake. I tried not to look at the water racing by under the wing. The engine began to howl at an impossible pitch. The pilot was staring ahead at the glassy surface of

73

the lake and the shore of the lake that was now rushing at us. "God-damn. Goddamn! There is no wind in this son bitchin' country. If you didn't want wind, it'd be all over ya. Gotta rock it to get off." He put the plane over on one pontoon; alternated first one then the other. We finally lifted off. This was my first time in a plane of any kind. I had nothing to say and stayed focused intently on the shore-line racing past. There was too much noise for talking, anyhow. He banked the plane sharply and turned north and east for Basswood. I saw organic patterns of swamps, ridges, and long fingers of water curving off to the north as far as I could see.

I felt very professional as I sat in my Olympian throne. Imag-ine being flown in! By the time we arrived at Peterson's, I was full of enthusiasm for how great it was to be a guide. There was a small group gathered on the dock at Pete's. We circled once, then came in low over the middle of the bay, heading straight in, and roared up to the dock. I saw Joe standing there, and a couple of the main-tenance crew. The apparent reception committee was exactly in keeping with my assessment of the importance of the moment. I assumed that Joe had actually put in a special request for me, so when I saw him, I grinned and waved. Joe stared, then looked be-yond me at the pilot, "Where'n hell's the booze?" he said. A box of bottles appeared at the door of the plane. "Here you go, Joe. Big party, huh?" Joe snorted, didn't even look up as he grabbed a fifth of whiskey from the box and walked off the dock. I picked up my pack and walked back of the lodge to the guide's shack. The magic slipped away.

Two days later, we started on the first of the side trips. Joe had already picked the three canoes and packed the camping gear at the Border Lakes warehouse. The gear was brought up Fall Lake and over the Four Mile Portage in Pete's truck. One of Pete's launches would tow us up the lake to North Bay. It was still early morning. We had already checked in at Jess Owen's, the Canadian ranger, for our park permits and fishing licenses. Joe was sitting in the back of the launch, up against a stack of packs staring out at the three canoes. A squat figure in a red and black checkered wool shirt, with a red bandanna tied over the top of his head, he looked neither happy nor sad to be there. He issued no invitation to conversation.

There were four men in the party; one of them had been at Pete's before. He went over and sat down by Joe and launched into animated stories of last year's trip. Joe was not impolite. He listened carefully, but had shifted his gaze to stare at a spot about eighteen inches in front of the speaker's face. His face was impassive and he said nothing in return. You simply knew, without being able to prove it, that he was somewhere else. Eventually the fisherman finished his story and got up and sat on the bench.

At North Bay, the launch dropped us off. It disappeared in a wall of sound down the channel, leaving the three canoes sitting in middle of a tiny back bay. When I loaded my canoe I had balanced it carefully with two heavy food packs behind the yolk, and two personal packs and fishing tackle forward. The canoe rode slightly down in the stern. Joe was packed and ready, too. He sat rolling a cigarette as he waited for the third canoe to get settled in. Joe looked like he was resting, he knew I had been to Isabella several times before. Without looking up, he said, "Go ahead, kid."

I took my crew out first and we worked our way up through the narrow channel in the lily pads. I was especially pleased to be leading the group. In Joe's presence it was the difficult to demonstrate that you knew anything at all. His moves were generally simpler and required less effort than mine. There was not a lot of talk so there was no subtle way that I could tell stories that gave hints about how much I really knew about all the lakes I had been in. In any case, I did know this route. I could look like a real professional here.

The brown water seemed only a few inches deep, but looks are deceptive, and in actuality you could not touch bottom with paddle or pole. The particles of mud held in suspension may have looked like bottom, but I had seen men sink in over their heads in what seemed to be six inches of brown water. Each paddle stroke stirred the mud, bringing swirls of it to the surface. We worked upstream in the morning glare. There was a faint odor of decay stirred up by our progress.

Every once in a while we would slip up close to a large pike lying just under the water. The fish would give a huge swirl as he streaked off, trailing a cloud of mud in his wake. I liked to think they were sunbathing, just lying up on the surface to warm themselves. Apparently, there are no eagles or hawks large enough to pose a threat to this habit. Sometimes you encountered them sunbathing in the middle of large lakes.

We approached the first beaver dam. It was about four feet high, constructed entirely of mud and short sections of logs. The dam rose in a graceful curved line that completely bisected the channel. There was a substantial torrent of water over at one end where some disgruntled canoeists had made a small breach. We headed straight for it, and my party stood up in the bow of our canoe in his new khaki pants. He stepped out without holding onto the canoe. The canoe shot back in response and left him standing, both feet together, on the large log slanting down the face of the dam. He began to move, slowly at first, then accelerating in his progress down the log. There was not even time to reach out for support as he disappeared from view. When he finally rose from the watery depths in a rose from the depths in a great cloud of aromatic mud, Joe smiled around the cigarette. "Loon shit, all you want for free," he joked. I brought the canoe up, and the man used it like a platform to heave his torso out of the water. From the irritated expression on his face, you could tell that he was searching for someone else to blame for the experience. When he saw the grinning faces around him, he thought the better of it. He took off his shirt, rinsed it as best he could, wrung it out, and put it on again. We got out on each side of the canoe and stood knee deep in mud as we pulled it up and over two logs placed in the spillway. We then floated in the pond behind the dam, waiting for the others in the hot morning sun.

If I had been the guide, I would have been standing in the spillway hurrying each canoe over. If the group were too slow about it I would personally heave each canoe over the drag logs. Joe sat down below the dam in the last canoe, watching and resting. The two tourists were terribly awkward and took forever to get out of his canoe. One even tried to keep his feet dry, which slowed things down even more. Joe acted as if we had all the time in the world. People talked and joshed each other; no one became irritated or upset.

I knew that we had two good portages and a small lake to cross before we reached Isabella and its black bass. As Joe finally began pulling his canoe over the dam, I spun our canoe around and headed upstream. My impatience was showing. Two more dams and we reached the first portage. I had the canoe on my back just as the next canoe came around the corner. I could easily make two trips with our gear and be back for a third to help them. I'd get these people moving. As I reached the other side of the short portage, I heard my party running behind me. I turned and could see he had no pack on his back and he was out of breath, "Pat, Joe didn't stop here, he just kept on going" We both trotted back, reloaded the canoe, and followed their path through the flattened swamp grass. The stream was tiny, less than five feet wide in some places. It wound back and forth in a deep channel through a narrow valley. We pulled over several more beaver dams and waded up one shallow riffle, pulling the canoe behind us. The eventual portage into Isabella was little more than a lift over.

That night we camped on a snug little campsite, midway down the lake on the east shore. It had been a very good day. The party had caught some good fish and went to bed early to miss the mosquitoes circling the fire. "Joe, how did you know that route?" I asked. I thought for a minute he wasn't going to answer. "I trap beaver up here, kid. A lot of times you don't have to portage if you just look real close." There was a long pause. "Always go round if ya can. Easy outlaw way of travelin'. "

The next day, I took a long look at the topographic map. I noticed for the first time how many lakes were connected by small streams and swampy areas. Over the next ten years, I found a half dozen of these "outlaw" routes. Each of them saved portaging; each also gave you a sense of being with the country, of going around instead of through each difficult pass.

It took much longer for me to adopt Joe's style of being easy with time and with his body. Our next side trip was also for bass, this time into Meadow Lake. One of the three portages into Meadow Lake was over a high ridge, then through two swamps. It was roughly a mile long. The portage occupied a special place among my contemporaries. As a matter of pride, it had to be done with a pack plus canoe. According to the rules of the young man game, at no time could the canoe be set down. Joe started first. To my surprise, he carried only his canoe. By the time I was ready, he was already moving smoothly up over the high ridge. I had my pack on and quickly rolled the canoe up and over my head. I shot the two paddles forward into the bow to give balance, and then I was off in a fast trot. I imagined the envy and admiring glances as I made swift progress to the ridge. I was panting by the time I hit the top; the pack straps were cutting off circulation in both arms. The mosquitoes found me as I entered the first swamp and easily pierced my blue cotton shirt, now wet with sweat. By this point, I was holding the canoe yolk off of one shoulder by tilting the canoe slightly. Both arms had begun to tingle, so I'd alternate letting one hang down while the other was above the head holding on to the thwart. I was only halfway. I was surprised then to catch a glimpse of Joe's feet and the stern of his canoe. I could see that he had put his bow between two jack pine growing close together. The canoe rested with its stern on the ground and the bow resting gently about ten feet off the ground. Joe had stepped out from under the canoe and was rolling his shoulders and swinging his arms as he glanced up at me. "Hi ya, kid. How come you hurry so much?" There was no disapproval in the voice, just a flat question. I would be forty years old before I finally learned that portaging really had nothing to do with proving yourself as a man.

Simple lessons are mainly taught without words. For example, one time we had to figure out Joe's kitchen was often an art form, more often than not the result of his having to overcome a specific problem. For example, one time he had to figure out what to do with a large boulder in the middle of the kitchen. His solution was to build the fireplace up so that the boulder became a backdrop. The wind pushed the flames into the boulder, giving the group more heat for cooking. Smaller rocks held the fire grate. I remember there were two large flat rocks; one on either side of the fireplace. that served as working tables to keep utensils off the ground. Off to one side and upwind, there was a poncho that held the pots and pans in close proximity to the working table and fire grate. Joe could not tolerate ashes falling in his working area and would rotate the entire arrangement if the wind shifted. When the fire was lit, he would then take a bar of soap and carefully wash his hands. That ritual would be repeated several times while he cooked. There were no wasted motions. Joe was a true professional and very deliberate in everything he did.

That summer, many of the commercial canoe trips included two guides. This was always useful because each had usually worked out slightly different ways of doing things. We each had a hundred small inventions for making things go more efficiently. Jim Santineau was one of my favorite partners. His father, Francis, a French Canadian, was one of the old line canoe guides. Two of his sons, Jim and his brother, Joe, were just beginning their guiding careers. It was hard to believe that the two brothers were even from the same gene pool. Joe was a huge hulk topped off with jet-black hair; he looked rather like an Indian. Jim, on the other hand, had sandy red hair and only stood 5'6". He weighed 140 pounds in wet wool socks. That is about what a personal pack plus an eighteen foot canoe weighs. However, it was also about the weight of the average French voyageur. Jim claimed it was a definite advantage to be "compact," especially if you were going to spend a lot of time in a canoe. He often spoke of my size as being a handicap. When he called me "Moose," he somehow enunciated it in a pitiful way.

For someone so small, Jim was jammed packed with very strong opinions. He was convinced, in advance, that whatever he did was obviously in the preferred way. This extended down to include very small things. For example, he insisted that for pancakes, the whites of eggs had to be beaten separately. If you allowed him to get away with it, he would launch into a long discourse about his French ancestors and their worshipful approach to cooking with eggs. He swore his pancakes were lighter and better than others. We never resolved this debate, but I observed him many mornings sitting out in the rain, separating yokes from whites. The grin on his face communicated his feeling that he represented a superior culture and didn't mind being observed by barbarians.

He may have been right about the pancakes, but I never accepted his strange belief in the virtues of a double-bitted axe as necessary tool for wilderness survival. We had nightly contests, each of us rushing out of camp in opposite directions "to make camp wood." My technique was to find a dead tree about as thick as my arm and place one end between two trees growing about two feet apart. The camp would be surrounded by the sounds of axe blows from one direction and snapping tree trunks from the other. Each of us carefully eyed the size of the pile brought by the other, making comments about its poor quality. I cast frequent aspersions about pint sized Frenchmen with unknown Indian contributors that required such a big axe. His allusions were to moose sized persons of dubious Scandinavian and Irish ancestry that were so limited in culture as to not yet have learned to use the tools of their civilized betters.

Jim was an artist with rain tarps. He would never admit that he had learned it from his father, but implied that the skill was yet another manifestation of superior genes and culture. He used the canvas tarps that we all carried, which ranged in size from 8 x 10 feet, for a small group to 10 x 12 feet for large gatherings, but his version had grommets every three feet so it could be tied off at any angle. An effectively employed rain tarp means the difference between merely surviving the rain and wind to being comfortable.

Given a heavy wind, we might set a canoe on its side and tie the bow to one tree and stern to another. Then we'd tie the eight-foot edge of the tarp off on the top thwart of the canoe. Depending upon the availability or the spacing for trees around the kitchen, we might require another five or six alder poles. These had to range in size from six to twelve feet long. Jim would disappear with his double-bit axe, and I would unsheath my belt knife. I had learned as a boy that if you climb partway up a stout alder and swing your feet out, the tree would gently lower you to the ground. If you straddled it to keep it bent, you could run your knife into the grain where it bowed. The wood simply melted as you pressed the blade home. You could fell a tree of astonishing girth this way; each looked as if it were slashed with an axe. Jim refused to learn the trick, mentioning it was not in keeping with the dignity of his ancestry to climb trees and then disembowel them.

In setting up the tarp, we would first cross two twelve-foot poles about at ten feet and tie them off with a short piece of rope. We'd stand the crossed poles up and loop twenty feet of rope at the corner of the tarp over it, then run it to a nearby tree. The other corner of the tarp was treated in a similar fashion with a second pair of crossed poles. At this point, all of the kitchen packs would be brought in and stowed in the back of the shelter. The dry wood was stored in the canoe itself. Two more poles were used to lift the outside edges at about the midpoint of the tarp. The effect was a Baker tent design. The heat from the fire on its outside edge reflected back from the rear slope and kept the whole place reasonably warm and quite dry. A pot of soup and a few sitting logs could make a miserable day downright comfortable. It was a great relief to be in a canoe during a driving rainstorm knowing that in another hour or two we'd be in camp with the tarp up.

Each guide worked out some small artistry. My father had a gift for fishing that seemed almost magical sometimes. He could read lake bottoms while standing on the shore. If you are a fisherman, especially one looking for large lake trout, then that gift has real meaning. Landlocked salmon often weighed fifteen pounds and could go up to and over thirty. Reading a lake bottom meant that you could pretty well figure out where these giant fish could be found. Lake trout only live in certain lakes: those deep enough to maintain an even temperature during the heat of summer. Ordinarily, this meant a deep lake, and this in turn usually meant a good sized lake.

My continuing education concerning lake trout occurred on a trip to the basin of lakes around McIntyre. Mr. Marhoefer had arranged this trip to introduce his son Erik to big fish, especially big lake trout. For this reason he demanded two guides, one for each canoe for a ten day trip. My father sometimes used his vacation time to sign on as a guide; this was one of those times. We had never worked together on a canoe trip before, so both of us approached it very carefully. I knew the routes and he did not. But he was my father, and I obviously could not take charge of the trip. It was interesting the way it eventually worked out. We learned to occupy a different space, but maintain our respect for what the other was doing.

We were moving through a series of small unnamed lakes to the south and east of the basin. My father had never been in this section of the Quetico before. Erik and I rushed from one small lake to another with my father and Marhoefer trailing along behind. The two older men had an endless supply of stories and seemed to enjoy each other's company. As they finally pulled in to a portage, Erik and I would be waiting impatiently for them. They allowed us to take their extra packs, but casually ignored other efforts to speed up their progress. Marhoefer was a huge bear-shaped figure with a wreath of grizzled gray hair and a bald pate. A pause of any duration was a signal for him to sit down and light his pipe. He did that now as the four of us stood in the muskeg at the edge of a tiny pond less than half a mile in diameter. Erik and I had just dropped their packs into their canoe, our third trip on the portage. Marhoefer seized the moment, and from the cloud of smoke asked, "What do you think, Pat? Anything in a pothole like this?" My father put his hand in the water and looked around as he lit a cigarette. "Trout," he said. "There are small lake trout in here." He turned to me, "What do you think?" I was stunned. My father was asking me whether we should stop and fish in this beaver pond! Here we were, trying to "make time" and get out of this muskeg country by dark, these old two graybeards were talking about catching lake trout in a beaver pond! However, Marhoefer had come to fish. My father was saying there were fish here. I knew I had to back down from an argument that I could not possibly win. I also knew that we would be here for hours and probably end up pitching a camp somewhere in the swamp. I turned and looked at the lake. "Trout? I've been through here five times and never even seen a fish. I've never even heard of anyone fishing here. Why trout?" The men were already getting out the trout rods and rigging up. "Feel the water. That's cold, real cold. It's coming from springs. Any of the lakes here in the basin that are cold could have lake trout in them."

He and Marhoefer both had big grins on their faces as Dad got into the canoe and shoved off. Apparently the discussion was over. "Okay, Erik, let's follow these two old-timers while they troll for trout in the lily pads." We hung back out of range, but did not bother to take out the fishing gear that sat in the top of our personal packs. The rod case remained lashed to the gunwales. They paddled out of the bay and into the center of the lake. The water was clear; you could see Marhoefer's KB spoon drop for a long time as it sank out of sight. They were still talking as Dad paddled slowly in a large circle out in the center of the lake. We drifted just within heckling range, with Erik lying back against the packs. Marhoefer's pole suddenly arched, and the star drag reel began to sing its fish song. Erik and I became very organized as we tried to find rod, reel, and tackle without tipping over the canoe.

Each trout weighed precisely three pounds. All were the same size, beautifully colored and very cold to the touch. We caught a dozen and kept two for dinner that evening. They were caught in thirty to forty feet of water on light tackle. Erik and I just barely managed to get the two smiling old-timers over the half-mile portage to Side Lake before dark. We camped on the south end of the lake on a rocky point. The fire was being lit just as the sun disappeared behind a sheer rock cliff.

The elders allowed the young men to set up camp. They leaned up against a log, sipping their whiskey and water. Both were tired; we had been up and traveling shortly after dawn that day. There was a nice quiet glow about the camp; not a lot of talking, but a sense that things had gone absolutely right. On more trips, the group process turns a corner of some kind and everything becomes more positive. Sometimes it happens on the last night. Sometimes, with certain people, it never happens. On this trip it was the third day when it happened, and we were only on the edge of the trout basin.

Side Lake is only a mile or two long and quite narrow, with high rock ridges running north and south on both sides of the lake. The next morning, it was very late when the sun finally came up over the ridge. All of us had slept in. The mist hung in shrouds over on the east shore as Erik and I moved around the fire, trying to be inconspicuous in our efforts to get the party into motion. Coffee finally brought both Dad and Marhoefer out of their tents. By prearranged plan, I began breakfast while Erik began dismantling their tent. Dad was sitting on his heels holding his coffee cup in both hands. He stood over six feet tall, very lean, his skin tanned almost black. His high cheekbones and distinctive nose, once broken in a brawl, gave his face a definite Indian cast. "Maybe we ought to check this lake out," he said. "It looks deep; it could be a good lake." He and Marhoefer talked quietly back and forth about the merits of spending a day where we were or going on to Sarah, a larger lake with the promise of larger fish. By the time the bacon was fried and the pancakes were done, the issue was decided. We would stay the morning on Side Lake to explore the potential for lake trout. We rigged the short heavy rods and the big star drag reels with their huge line capacity.

The south end of the lake proved to be very deep. Neither canoe had a strike. We reeled in. The two canoes drifted. None of us were saying much. Erik and I were both chagrined at having lost yet another day. Neither of us voiced this as a concern. Dad had a habit of reaching up with his right hand for the cigarettes in his shirt pocket, taking one out and lighting it without seeming to notice what he was doing. As we drifted, he went through his ritual, several times lighting up and staring thoughtfully up the narrow lake. "The trout are in here all right, but not in this end. This time of year they would be hanging around the reef up there in that narrow channel." Erik and I looked at each other and I laughed, "Which reef, Dad?" There was absolutely no reef showing anywhere. "It's down there, about fifty feet deep. See the point of land at the neck on the west side?" He pointed with his cigarette. "See that other point on the other side? Well, imagine how the bottom would look if you drained the water out. Those two points are connected by a ridge. That's your reef. That's where the trout will be." There was a respectful silence. The canoes drifted back up the lake, and Marhoefer sat staring up at the narrow neck in the middle of the long lake.

Dad was right about the trout being on a reef in the narrow neck. We found it by bouncing lead weights along the bottom. As the reef rose, we would reel in and then when you could no longer feel the bounce we'd let out line until we found the reef again. A fisherman has to stay in constant touch with things he cannot see. We found the lake trout, in the end, but did not keep any of them.

Two days later we were fishing off the face of the big cliff east of the narrows at Sarah Lake. When Dad came peddling into camp, Marhoefer was sitting in the front of the canoe with a stunned expression, staring at his bent fishing rod. They had been fishing with a Monel (metal) line in very deep water. Something struck that occupied them for thirty minutes before the pole gave way.

The summer slipped by quickly. By late August, the evenings were beginning to feel chilly. I had spent the last ten days with a party of three from Kentucky. John Plampf, his sister Marg, and their good friend Willi Willenbrink were young and adventurous. They had allowed me to talk them into a long trip to Kawa Bay. We had traveled north and east right through the Quetico and then off the edge of the map. We spent two days cutting a portage into McKenzie Lake where we caught some enormous Northerns. Then as the bad weather moved in, we turned and fled south. Heavy wind caught us as we entered the chain of lakes leading into Moose Lake. Line after line of huge rollers came straight into our bow. Dark clouds hung low over the islands. The canoes were side by side as we rode the waves. We were all pleased to be going in and planned an outrageous dinner when we arrived in Ely that night.

It was dark when we entered the narrow channel into the north end of Moose Lake. The truck from Canoe Country Outfitters would be waiting on the other side of the lake, all that was necessary was for us to get there. Ordinarily the wind died with the sunset, but not this time. If anything, it was blowing harder. I placed my personal pack face down in front of me and locked my knees into the leather straps, sitting low with my butt just resting against the front of the seat. This position provides stability while at the same time giving maximum leverage to the paddle.

We quartered our way to the left across the first long open

stretch. Each quartering tack brought us up against the eastern shoreline, a brief respite as we sponged out the water. We also chewed our way through enormous pieces of hardtack coated with peanut butter. Finally, we rounded the point. We could see the headlights from the truck at the landing. As we drew closer, it became clear that our pickup driver standing there in the headlights was Bill Rom, the owner of Canoe Outfitters. He was standing next to a long line of Duluth packs. I felt a twinge of sorrow for those unfortunates who would turn our canoes around and follow the storm into the night.

We landed and the party began emptying the canoes. I walked over to meet Bill, who was still standing by the packs. He shook the rain from his campaign hat. "So, what kind of a trip did you have?" He looked over at the party who were busy laughing and talking as they threw their packs into the back of the truck. He grinned, "Never mind, I can see you had a great trip. Did you make it to Kawa Bay?" A year ago Bill and my brother Mike and I had passed through Kawa Bay on our way east to Mack Lake. In fact, after that trip I began working regularly for Rom. We talked briefly about the trip, then he turned and motioned to the line of packs, "Here's a new outfit." I hardly paused. "Yeah, but who are the lucky people?" I asked. He took his hat off again, brushed his hair, then looked at me and laughed. "You."

"The hell you say. What do you mean, me?"

"I went to your ma and got you a clean outfit. You're packed for an eight day trip with that guy over there." He pointed to a figure standing in the shadows behind the truck. The wind whipped his poncho in swirls about him. I could not see his face. He made no effort to move forward to join us.

I turned to Bill in anger. "Goddammit, I've been in the bush ninety days this summer. We're going to have a big party tonight in town." Bill didn't say anything for a moment as he walked me away from the headlights, "This guy, Dr. Bob, has been waiting in Ely for you for five days. He was out with your buddy, Jim

Santineau. Jim told him about you, so he stayed so he could take a trip with you."

"What the hell sort of crazy things did he say about me? Jesus!"

Bill turned back to the truck. "Damned if I know. One more thing: he don't want to do a lot of talking."

"Sounds like a great trip: eight days with some guy who don't talk." I stamped off to say goodbye to my party, then proceeded with the task of loading the canoe bouncing in the waves that pounded into the shore.

Bill introduced us. As I shook Dr. Bob's hand I said, "I have a great job for you. Could you hold the canoe steady while I load it? It's a good chance to get rid of those dry socks." He smiled and nodded his head. A short, rather slight figure, he seemed entirely too frail for this environment. His hands were small and his handshake lacked the verve I had come to expect from those who expended so much to be in this place. The rain began just as we finished loading. It came slowly at first, and then in great sheets. Dr. Bob got in. I noticed that he crab-walked the gunwales and stayed off the packs, a very unusual move for a tourist to make. I waded out and shoved the canoe into the waves, and let the wind take us back down the lake. The rain worked its way down the sleeves of my rain jacket and then penetrated the shoulders and back. My wool shirt was soaked along with my canvas pants. I knew he had to be wet and cold. We said nothing as we moved out of the wind into the narrow channel into Newfound Lake. He sat bent forward, shrouded in his poncho and stroking to my fast pace. The rain slowed, but the wind made its own restless sounds as it slipped through the tops of the trees on either side of us.

It caught up with us as soon as we left the sheltered bay, splashing over black water with wind slicing the tops of the waves. I could hear the hissing sounds that waves make when they are big enough to force a canoe to broach. I had to sweep powerfully to compensate. I shouted above the wind, "We've got to camp soon, just beyond the point ahead." We crossed the lake slowly and landed on the lee side of the second point. The wind had shifted to the east and was enfilading the point. There was no protection here, but realistically, there were no other camps within our reach. The figure in the poncho picked up his personal pack and slowly climbed the ridge up into the wind. I double-packed our equipment to a camp sited in a slight depression. If you sat down, the wind roared just over your head. Huge black pines swayed and moaned all around the site.

I sheltered the fire pit with two packs; then used the pitch wood left from the Kawa Bay trip to start a fire. The flames bent in a sheet a foot above the ground and illuminated Dr. Bob slumped against a tree. He had thin, gaunt features; he followed me about with his eyes, but said nothing. He seemed exhausted. I rigged a rain tarp to break the wind and then prepared supper. First, split pea soup and fresh home baked bread forwarded by mother through Bill Rom. Then, thick slices of ham fried with fresh potatoes sliced very thin, and shrouded with a few diced onions. I said, "You okay? You look pretty cold. Why not come over here by the fire and let the tarp break the wind." He nodded, rose heavily, staggered slightly as he lifted his personal pack, and sat closer to the fire. We sat in a small circle of warmth as the wind bent the trees and moved the flames in sheets, first one way, then another.

My hands shook as I lifted the cup of soup. We each had several cups of soup in quick succession. He leaned back against one of the packs and said, "Would you share some brandy?" His way of speaking caught my attention. It was something I had not heard before; careful enunciation with a slight hint of an English accent. I looked at him more closely. He had fine features with a slightly boyish cast to them and carefully trimmed wet hair that was parted in the middle. I saw a very tired man of about fifty years. He filled the two tin cups with very precise movements. He corked the bottle and handed me my cup. Raising his own cup, he said, "Cheers," touched my cup and smiled for the first time. We worked our way through the brandy and the ham and potatoes with such intensity that we did not hear the wind slow, or then die. High above us the clouds still raced across the moon. I washed the dishes. We began a conversation that was to continue for over six years.

Dr. Bob lived in Wheaton, Illinois. It was only several years later that I ever heard what he did for a living. In this first conversation, I gathered that he lived in a strange world of expensive people. He had a butler. Evidently he was subjected to extraordinary pressures that he never detailed. Once a year he would leave the city and spend a month in the wilderness. Sometimes he would be a member of a group. Other times it would be just Dr. Bob and one or two guides. He had canoed in Maine and Manitoba. He had ridden on horseback through the Canadian Rockies and much of the Sierras. This was the first time he had come to Minnesota. On his trip with Jim Santineau, he had fallen in love with the pristine quality of the Quetico wilderness.

He sat staring into the fire, looking up only occasionally as he moved from describing the culture of a large metropolitan Chicago and then his trips into first one wilderness then another. It was very late when he returned to describing his reaction to the Quetico: "It is perfect, you know. In its own way, it is still all of one piece. This Canadian shield extends from here right to the western shore of Hudson Bay. There are no roads, nothing has been straightened out, and nothing has been cut or dammed. Our culture has not penetrated this place, or at least for only a thin distance. Its natural state . . . perfect, you see."

The storm blew itself out eventually. Up shortly after dawn the next day, I started the fire, made coffee, and waited for a sign of life from his tent. The wind was beginning to make telltale ripples across the water. A few of the maples experimented with their autumn color. It would be an early fall. The air was washed clean. My tent had dried in the morning sun, so I packed it and all of my personal gear. Then I went through all of the gear to see firsthand what had been packed for us. The sun was halfway through the morning when I placed the coffee cup by his tent door, from which there was a laugh, "Good morning, Jerry. You're up early."

That surprised me. "Yeah, well, I thought we might be moving." A hand groped for the coffee cup, followed by a face, "Marvelous day. Let's do travel; but why at dawn? How about a slow breakfast, then we will see what happens."

Thus began his gentle but persistent rebellion. It never encompassed central issues such as safety or comfort, his point of view usually emphasized the aesthetics of the experience. For example, breakfast was not a linear track one raced through in order to break camp as quickly as possible. "This is a beautiful place on the point," he said. "We should not hurry away from it. Could I have some hot water? When I come back, I will cook the breakfast. You are not allowed to do anything for the next hour." He laughed at my discomfort, pressed a cup of coffee into my hands, then turned and walked away with his hot water to shave.

Canoe parties began to stream by our campsite on their way to Prairie Portage. A guide from the Scout base recognized me and swung by to see if I was all right. I had no explanation for how it was nine in the morning and we had not even had breakfast yet. I lost immeasurable status for the obvious breach in procedure. I knew that evening, around their campfire, they would likely discuss my demise as a true voyageur, a victim of commercialism. I was no longer a true Courrier du Bois, runner of the woods.

I returned, stoked the fire, and waited impatiently for my "party" to get in motion. He appeared freshly shaved, clean suntan pants rolled up at the cuff to expose new moccasins. The expensive tailored red wool shirt he wore was topped by a beaming countenance. His hair was combed again and neatly parted in the middle. He looked like a 1930s ad from Abercrombie and Fitch. I started to get up, intending to start cooking, but he said, "No, sit. Breakfast is on me. After what you did last night, it is my turn. Fair is fair."

So deftly done. In less than a day, Dr. Bob had subtly altered the power structure between us. I was not upset about the change, just surprised. I sensed that on this trip there would be no long-range plan, no distant goal that would dictate our day-to-day movement. On this trip, each day was planned as it was that morning. "What do you feel like doing today?" he asked. He moved efficiently about the kitchen, using up all of the fresh eggs Bill had added to our food supply. He hummed a melody I had never heard before, then a brisk rendition of a song that was only a play on the small word "jada." He carefully ignored me as I squatted on my heels in impatient silence.

Ordinarily I would agree to a trip objective with the party before leaving the outfitting company. It would be reified at the custom office where we outlined the trip route. Given such a plan, each day's activities were preset. In some very real sense, most canoe trips were like military operations, very well planned and executed. The success of a trip was partially measured in accord with how well the plan was kept. But here was someone who was not going according to a plan. He had no interest in miles covered or number of portages carried. That first morning he also announced that while he loved to eat fish, he had absolutely no interest in catching them! On this, and all other trips, when I wished to cook fish, he would simply paddle while I sat in the front holding the fish rod.

The Dr. Bob revolution struck at the very heart of ancient canoeing traditions. Instead of a master plan dictating activities for the entire journey, there was a question. "Could we make a plan each morning or evening and just do what we feel like doing? Is that all right with you? Do we shatter the code of the Courrier du Bois if we travel hard some days and lie around and do nothing on others?" I sat there for a minute trying to assimilate this new path into my unconscious. I mumbled an unconvincing, "Well, yeah, oh sure, we can do that, but . . ." He interrupted with a grin. "Maybe there are some places you haven't been and we could go there; but the main thing is to take each day as it comes." He had found my Achilles heel! I brightened up at the suggestion of exploring new canoe routes. Most guided trips traveled the same well-known routes; and there were only about a half dozen such routes you could take on a five day trip. You could see on the maps that these routes left huge gaps between them, so you could not usually travel from one route to another. Doing this would require cutting your own portages and each campsite would have to be created on the spot. None of the commercial parties that I guided would be interested in finding a new path; it would interfere with fishing. No one even knew what kind of fish were in the off-route lakes.

I described an idea that I'd had for some time. I wanted to travel in a relatively straight course due west from Silent Lake through an unexplored chain to Kashipiwi, then through a series of creeks and small ponds to Joyce Lake. It seemed like a plan. We didn't necessarily have to complete it in one year. We could turn off at any point and return to Moose Lake in order to keep our appointment with Bill Rom. That day I sat in the bright morning sun, eating a breakfast cooked by someone other than myself, and thinking of lakes I had never seen. I hardly noticed the other boats streaming past our camp. We were already disengaged and on a different path from theirs. This new path felt very much like an old path: this man from Chicago had connected me to my childhood at Robinson Lake. We shared a yearning to be on a lake that no one had been before, and to find the perfect camp site.

We arrived at the ranger station at Bailey Bay late that afternoon. As we rounded the black-rock tipped point, we could see the white sand beach cutting a crescent far back into the bay. It was a picture, perfectly balanced by the red roofed ranger cabin with its red maple leaf flag set snug up against the ridge at one end of the bay. As we drew closer, we could see the well made-dock resting on its log cribbing. The window frames for the log cabin were painted white, and most amazing of all, the grass had been freshly mowed! Each ranger station along the border was constructed in a similar fashion. The Canadians who manned them were invariably polite, neatly dressed men who gave us our travel permits and sold us fishing licenses with minimum fuss (and at a great cost to their government). Each had a radio that could be used to call in fire fighters or rescue groups. They, and their families, maintained these tiny bastions of order, paint, and polite protocol at the every edge of the bush.

We landed far up the beach well away from the score of canoes from other parties being processed. After checking in, we walked slowly back to our canoe, our pace languid by comparison to the bustle and shouts of dozens of people getting ready to leave or just arriving. I pointed to a trail through the balsam grove. "That portage takes us to Burke Lake," I told him. "If we travel hard, we can be through it and up at the end of North Bay by evening. By noon tomorrow, we could be in the north arm of Silent Lake. From there, we'll travel due east. We won't travel very far, but when we are done we will have cut a new canoe route from Silence Lake to Kashipiwi. Best of all, we will see no one for several days. Nothing. Our own private wilderness."

I was not sure how Dr. Bob would react to the idea of a day and a half of hard travel. I was always in a particular hurry to move through a transition zone, and this was such a place. A transition zone is that narrow strip that lies between the roads and the deep bush. In the transition zones within the Quetico, the camps are overused. Each has a light tracery of discarded cigarette stubs and a sprinkling of trees scarred by axe cuts that served no real purpose. It is not because the campers are bad; it is just that there are too many of them. The pine needle duff is worn through to rock and dirt. The campsites no longer feel right.

By way of answer to my implied question, Dr. Bob quickened his pace. "All right, you have allowed me to rest for a day. Now I must pay a price. Today, tomorrow, many paddle holes, then much peace. Let's hurry; there is much to be done." Smiling and nodding to the paddlers coming and going along the beach, he strode purposefully to our canoe. He picked up the bread pack, and swung it expertly on his shoulders. "And now," he said, "my personal pack, with its sacred medicine. Gently please." He adjusted the tump line across the top of his head and headed out in a good imitation of the voyageurs' shuffle. Given the huge bulk of the Duluth pack topped with his personal pack, the only thing I could see of him were the neatly rolled up cuffs of his suntans and his shiny new boots. I thought I caught a hummed rendition of Jada as he disappeared.

Soon we were back in motion. He set a creditable pace through Burke Lake, about one stroke every three seconds. We arrived in North Bay just before dusk. He pitched his own tent. Then, while I prepared the meal, he mixed a drink of hot orange juice and gin: "A proper drink for entering the bush," he declared. "Cheers." After dinner, he watched as I carefully cut an alder bush into a ten-inch handle with a short fork at one end, then folded a metal "chore girl" over the forked end and tied it off with some twine. I presented it to him. "For the true voyageur, who must paddle and scrub his way through the bush." He sighed. "Perfection lasts only a moment; black pots go on forever," he replied. We bought the pot of hot water previously used to warm the dinner plates to a boil and evenly divided it into two pots: one for soapy water and one to rinse. He worked his way through the dishes as I covered the packs and put together the small pile of dry wood for tomorrow's fire. By the time I had carried the canoe a few feet up from the lake and turned it over, he had the dishes turned upside down on the kitchen tarp. As I approached, he reached over into his personal pack. "In Wheaton, Illinois, the proper code of conduct says that the end of a fine day should be celebrated with a fine brandy." He filled half the tin cup with a flourish from a strangely shaped bottle. "One of the few good things that can be said of Napoleon. He was said to prefer this particular brandy. Cheers." He sat sipping the brandy and listening to the quiet sounds that came with the evening. "Tell me about the country we are going to," he asked.

"Well, first thing tomorrow will be a series of small lakes and short streams. They will take us out of North Bay. All the portages are short ones. By, noon we should be getting into the high country with its steep ridges and deep lakes with clear water. It is beautiful country. Both ends of the country we will explore have those high ridges, glaciated rock, and deep water. I expect our new route to look like that, too." Dr. Bob was one of those rare persons who did not seem to guard what he was feeling. He would often smile before he talked. He smiled now as he toasted me, again. "To our adventure. But, Courrier du Bois, what if you cannot find a way through there?" He laughed at my startled reaction. "I see the thought hasn't crossed your mind. All the better." He did this sort of thing often: a quick darting flight to an idea standing in the shadows. Often I did not understand the content of these flights, but they never seemed shaped to hurt or embarrass. I came to accept this way of talking as normal when with Dr. Bob.

We were up at dawn the next day and moving on the water within an hour and a half. Dr. Bob seemed to enjoy the idea of "making time" and had his tent folded and packed by the time I had cooked the oatmeal and dehydrated fruit (put out to soak the night before). As he washed the dishes, I carried the packs down to the canoe. We were in good form as we threaded the islands with campers just lighting their fires. He began to sing some songs I had never heard before, many from the "Princeton class musical of 1923." He swept his wool hat off in a low bow and turned. "You have the rare privilege of hearing the songs rendered by the author himself," he said. We spent the morning moving through West and then Noon Lake. Dr. Bob sang his songs and talked about the world of the Princeton undergraduate. I enjoyed the music, but it also made me feel slightly awkward. I could not join in, having been previously certified by several school teachers as entirely innocent of any musical talent.

We had lunch at the end of the portage in the stand of jack pine at the Noon Lake campsite. The trees here were all evenly spaced along a gently sloping gravel bar that shelved into the water. This was a peaceful place that always gave me a good feeling. The year before, I had crossed the lake and cut a portage into a no name lake that was full of black bass.

Even though we made two trips on each portage, we were still making very good time. The wind had been pushing steadily against us as we moved north. After lunch, it continued to increase. By the time we reached the south tip of Silence Lake, heavy waves were pounding into the rocks at the end of the portage. The wind whipped the bow of the canoe around, forcing me into a delicate half pirouette there on the flat rocks of the shore. I placed the canoe well back in the trees and walked back with Dr. Bob to pick up the remaining packs. "We may have to wait for this to blow over," I warned. "It would be heavy going out there in the open water." He walked along behind me, the wind whipping the trees over our heads in restless motion. I talked of the possibility of stopping here, out of the wind, and making a fire and a pot of soup. Dr. Bob didn't pick up on that idea, so we put on the packs and started back. Black clouds were now rolling over the north horizon, giving the whole picture an ominous cast. You could smell the rain coming. The loons were riding the wind and calling down their wild staccato cry. Loons get excited by a storm moving in and have a special call just for the occasion—a crazy, wavering cry that borders on a scream. We stood at the edge of the lake listening to the wind and the loons.

I felt very lonely suddenly and wished I were somewhere else. The question was, could Dr. Bob hold up his end in such waves? If he let up, we would broach, and fill up. It would be best to move back into the brush and set up a Siwash camp somewhere out of the wind. Then another surprise from Dr Bob: he stood smiling at the mass of black rollers and whitecaps, pounding the shore. "Jim Santineau would probably just go right down the middle."

Then he turned to watch me as I struggled with my young wounded manhood. "Well, hell, I suppose we can do it. You want to?"

I put the canoe in the water. Dr. Bob waded out waist deep to hold it in place and away from the rocks. I ferried the packs and then held the canoe while he got into the bow. "Ready?" He held his paddle in the air in salute. His poncho, unhinged, whipped about him like a demented thing as the bow rose and fell several feet. I shouted, "Pull!" and turned the bow into the wind. Dr. Bob was pulling hard, but the slow, 3-second stroke would let the wind turn us broadside to the rocks without ever leaving the shore. "Pull, pull, pull," I shouted as I raised the pace to one stroke per second. We hung there. Very slowly we moved away from the rocks behind us. Then finally, we moved away from the shore.

With the first wave, we had taken in some water, but, as we began to quarter to the left it finally stopped. "Dr. Bob, that's great. Can you keep it up like that?" I asked. He was shouting and singing in a foreign language as we moved into the lines of black water and rode over them one by one. I had my knees in the straps of the Duluth pack in front of me and put every ounce of energy from legs and back to arms and paddle. We were making steady progress to the first point on the west shore. Now we were both howling into the wind, grinning at each other and laughing. We were all right!

We stopped in the lee of the point and sponged a few quarts of water out. We had peanut butter and hard tack from the lunch pack for fuel. Then there was the long pull past the walleye reef in the middle of the lake and past the fine campsite on the island at the north end. Knees, backs, arms, and canoe were welded into one unit as we inched by the tiny island. As we rounded the last point on the west shore, we could see the deep ridge of the west arm just a few hundred yards away. The ridges were too high for the wind driving from the north to have any purchase on us. Dr. Bob turned, his hair a tangled mass and his face illuminated by a small boy's chortling cry. "We did it!" he shouted. He lifted his paddle in both hands over his head and shook it at the wind. Princeton was far from here! The urbane city dweller was set aside for the moment, and there was instead this middle-aged man signaling his triumph to the wind. The new suntans were no longer creased and immaculate. The knees were ringed with sand and grime from the ribs and planking where he had knelt to battle waves and wind.

In the west arm, the wind roared across the ridge high above our heads. We found a small level spot that could be made into a campsite. Together we moved some small logs and then leveled the ground for two tent sites. Within an hour and a half the fire was going and dinner was cooking. He sat by the fire with two tin cups in front of him, humming his strange songs, as he circled from butter tin to sugar sack to bottle of rum, and finally added a dollop of hot water. "A drink to the wind. Cheers." He collapsed against a huge log, sporting a wicked grin that surmounted the wet clothes and wet hair plastered to his skull. He glanced up at the trees still dancing high up on the ridge, and said, "God, what a great day!"

"Yeah, I remember last night saying how easy it was going to be. Sometimes the electricity comes in wrong." He leaned forward, holding his cup in both hands. Then, speaking softly, more to himself than to me, he began to share. "In those waves today I found a place I had not been before. In the city, you lose that place. Most of us spend most of our whole lives lost—lost in a fog of symbols, schedules, words. But today was for real. What you could see in those waves was what you got–outcome totally up to you. And we did it!" He gave me a huge smile.

The next morning Dr. Bob reinstated his subtle sabotage of planned time schedules. The coffee by his tent door and a description of the cloudless morning brought only low moans from inside the tent. "Courrier de Bois, my mind is willing. At your command it will arise, but, sad to say, without the body." There followed a carefully negotiated late-morning start and an agreement to stop at the first beautiful camp we encountered in our movement west. I was having difficulty containing my excitement about what we were about to do. The hand reached for its third cup of coffee before he emerged from his tent. Baking powder biscuits, bacon, and the last of the fresh eggs finally produced the resurrection. We managed to be on the water by mid-morning. As we stroked slowly down the west arm, the sun was already warm against our backs.

I could already see where the portage would be cut to the first lake. There was a notch at the end of the bay. That would be where the creek left Silence to flow into a tiny lake about a quarter of mile beyond. I suggested that Dr. Bob wait for me as I set off with the axe to find the best place to lay the portage. He slumped in a graceless heap against a pine and reached for a cigarette.

I strode up the small ridge. As soon as I was out of sight, I broke into a slow run. I moved over fallen trees and around a small swamp, working my way up a small ridge. I could hear the sound of water moving in the creek below me. My excitement mounted. I kept looking ahead for my first glimpse of the lake. I was sweating freely now and kept moving the rolled bandanna on my forehead, looking for a dry spot that was no longer there. I was up on the ridge now and able to move at almost a dead run. There was no need to blaze trees marking the route. There was no sound except my own heavy breathing as I followed the glaciated spine. I caught a glimpse of water ahead and then broke out of the stand of birch on a hill overlooking a tiny lake. It was not even as large as Robinson. I squatted on my heels examining the treasure below me. I could see the hills' contour, further to the west, suggesting a larger body of water. I squatted for a long time. I felt as if gentle fingers were reaching out from me to touch everything I could see.

After a long time I rose, unsheathed the axe, and began to blaze the east face of the larger trees. I also broke clumps of alder brush as I moved back to the canoe. The trail needed to be about four feet wide to permit the canoe to slip through, with a blaze marking about every twenty feet. I had been gone almost an hour by the time I worked my way back to the canoe. Dr. Bob was up on the ridge picking blueberries from the high bushes and trying to act unconcerned. "So then, do we have a northwest passage? Berries for tonight's biscuits." He tipped his hat to show me.

"Yes, there is a pretty little lake over there, and behind that, another, larger lake where we will make a camp." I wondered if he could sense the excitement at the edge of my voice. As we started back up the ridge, I still had not stopped talking. "It's got a nice rock shoreline, with a lot of cedar and birch," I was telling him. From behind me, Dr. Bob fought to keep from laughing. "Well, that sounds pretty unusual for this part of the country," he said. I rushed on with the canoe, and in my haste, lost the blaze trail several times. Then I had to stand patiently in company with an attending cloud of mosquitoes while Dr. Bob circled around me and finally located the next blaze.

The lake lay below us only a few hundred yards away. The surface was metal smooth, and it had a tiny clutch of lily pads at one end. To me it seemed a perfect world, hot and silent, a tiny round place framed by jagged ridges. An inverted world reflected in the water was as real and detailed as the one in which we stood: The place was so perfect that it gave you two pictures of itself. We turned and worked our way down a notch in the ledge to the lake. My shoulders hurt like they always did, even for a short carry. I was slightly out of breath as I burst through the heavy stand of alder and came to the muskeg at the end of the lake. This was my personal lake. I wanted to celebrate the occasion in some way, but didn't quite know how to express it. A big tamarack lay stretched far out into the water, its huge root system bleached white. The trunk and limbs were polished bone. I climbed up on the trunk and walked over the water as if on a bridge. As I continued, the trunk began to sway up and down, keeping time to my steps. Without pausing, I moved with the rhythm of the tree. When I stopped, I continued bobbing up and down following its motion. On the next upsurge, I lifted the canoe and turned to set it down across my thighs. The bow touched the water for balance as I slid the canoe into the lake. I tied it off, and walked back feeling a little embarrassed. I tried not to look at Dr. Bob. I had laid claim to my lake. I didn't want him to say anything that might mock me. I had my head down as I walked by, and heard Dr. Bob softly say, "I don't think I've ever seen anything quite like that before." He stood looking at the canoe tied to the great hulk of the tree, ripples moving from it out into the lake.

Later as we pushed the fully loaded canoe away from the log, neither of us spoke. Paddles tied in a single motion, the canoe was pushing lines out from the bow. There was no sound except the drip of water as the blade moved forward again. We moved forward to search for a likely spot for the next portage. This time there was no labor saving ridge to follow and we had to cut the portage yard by yard. By the time we had lunch on the second lake, we both felt tired. The lake lay on a north-south axis and our freshly cut portage trail had come out on its upper end. Dr. Bob lay back against the bank watching two loons swim away from our location, "The reception committee has taken some offense," he joked. "Perhaps it is the unsanitary condition that comes from no bath, no laundry." He glanced in my direction, "And no rest for three days." For no reason I could put my finger on, I found this mildly irritating.

"Jesus, Dr. Bob, it's early. You want to stop and camp in the middle of the day?" He looked at me for a moment, and grinned, "Who would know? Even if tortured, I would never admit that one day you did stop early to make camp."

Actually, I could think of no real reason for going on, except that was how it had always been done. Once the canoe was in the water and loaded, it meant traveling as far as possible until the hour just before darkness. Each day followed the same master plan. This made it almost impossible to fall victim to the impulse to go for a swim, or pause without the vague sense of falling behind. "It would feel good to stop early, take a bath, and do our laundry," he continued. I reluctantly agreed. We moved down the lake along the east shore, looking for a campsite. He lily dipped as he talked more to himself than to me. "Yes—doing is good," he declared. He stopped paddling and faced the high ridge to his left and, raising his voice, and shouted, "But, my Lord, BEING IS BETTER!" The message moved back and forth across the lake.

We worked our way slowly along the shore, looking for a campsite. "I notice your candle is on each night; do you read?" he asked me. I could see that across the lake there was a smooth rock shelf sloping down into the water, with a small grove of balsam behind it. I turned the canoe and we made our way slowly toward it. "Yeah, I read for a little while each night." He saw the rock, too, and picked up the pace with his paddle. "What kind of things do you read?" he asked.

"A little Emerson, and right now, it's the Old Testament. I was told that studying it is a good way to begin an education. But, I don't know—ahhh . . ." Dr. Bob had stopped paddling and turned in surprise. I felt acutely embarrassed, "I guess I need to read it a lot more because I don't really understand much," I added. "But in some places, it's very well written." Dr. Bob had turned back, and we were pulling hard for the ledge now.

"Which parts did you especially like?"

"Genesis, the first few chapters."

He nodded his head. The pace continued to increase. We could both see that it would be a good place to make camp. I took my paddle like a coal shovel and dug deep to make the bow shoot up out of the water at each stroke. Now we were both pulling and the canoe was rocking at each stroke. We shouted, "Hoo!" at each stroke; shouting it at the hills for the sheer joy of being there, in that place. Echoes ringing back, and ripples spreading out from the storm center, we disrupted the entire end of the lake as we claimed it for ourselves. I swerved the bow at the last moment, and we drifted broadside up to the docking ledge.

This had to be a perfect camp; there was even a perfect kitchen up by a small ledge that ran close to the water. Dr. Bob called from further up the slope, "Two fine tent sites, caribou moss all over." The familiar ritual began again. In a short time, the kitchen was laid out and the tents were in place. I walked about in my clean wool socks and moccasins, collecting the evening supply of cooking wood from the shoreline. Dr. Bob was in his familiar position against a tree with his personal pack beside him and a pile of books on the ground. I changed clothes and sat down on the ledge by the canoe soaping my canvas pants, socks, and wool shirt. After soaking under a rock, they were scrubbed against the smooth face of the ledge, rinsed, and hung on a bush to dry. I stripped and soaped myself down as I stood knee-deep in the coffee brown water. The water down by my feet seemed ice cold; only the surface felt warm. I dove down into it, flutter-kicking hard toward the clouds of crystal bubbles coming from hands thrust in front of me. The cold rushed along my body and made me gasp as I hit the surface, moving very fast, and transitioned into a crawl stroke that lasted until the shock passed. I moved back into a powerful crawl with my back arched to lift the shoulders into a fast driving stroke, and skimmed the surface of the water just at eye level. Body driving through the water as the flutter-kick and stroke moved into a smooth pattern, I experienced a moment of perfect harmony with the water, no sense of cold, no sense of stroking or kicking, all a part of the same thing, a part of the water.

Then the moment passed and there was slight fatigue, a sense of stroking, and a separate sense of kicking. A separate sense of breathing hard. I gave one more celebratory shout, then I rolled over, and kicked slowly back toward shore. Shouting always did, and still does, seem the only language for that sense of total focus. My usual focus felt like a stream of disconnected thoughts that could not be shepherded into coherence. But sometimes as when I was swimming that day, or in the storm of the day before, all senses become focused. They all fuse together just for a tiny moment: the world out there, the world in here, and one's body forming a perfect triangle.

I put on clean clothes and walked up to where Dr. Bob sat against the tree. "Here is a book written by another race of people about the Creation, the same topic as Genesis." He handed me a tiny, blue, cloth-covered book embossed in gold lettering, *Celestial Song.* "This is the Hindu version of how it all started," he told me. "In its own way it is also beautifully written." I found a place to sit and opened the book. I had never spent an afternoon in the bush reading a book. We repeated this ritual many times in the years that followed. We'd travel hard to someplace beautiful enough to make us stop, then we'd rest, read books, and talk while we paddled or sat around in camp.

We sat against a log by the kitchen fire, dishes put away, drinking a Dr. Bob (rum, hot water, butter, and a touch of sugar). The treetops to the west were black spear points holding up a mass of red and pink clouds. "Dr. Bob, why do you come here?" I asked.

He laughed. "That's strange. My friends in Chicago ask me that all the time. I can never quite seem to answer the question."

"Yes, but I'd be really interested," I persisted. He glanced at me, and then sat quietly for a moment.

"Well, it has something to do with yesterday," he began, "and with some moments today, too. Such moments occur in the city, too, but I find that the ones that occur here are more likely to be really special." I gave no sign that I understood.

"Well, let's say that there are peak moments. You go beyond words. Someone named Maslow has written about it. I'll send you his books if you like."

"Yes," I said, "I think I can understand that—but what is a peak moment?"

He nodded his head thoughtfully. "Yesterday in the waves and wind when we were yelling. For me, that was a peak moment. You can find it in many places: music, a fine painting, or a new idea. But they all have one thing in common; they do not last very long." I thought about that for some time. "It's just strange to think of finding peak moments in the same place that you find sweat,

105

mosquitoes, and swamps." He swept his cup across the horizon. "That sunset night there is my strongest counter-argument. By itself, it is a tiny peak moment. But you need neither liquor nor words to make it come alive."

"Why not just read about it, or go to a movie?"

A long pause. "Yes, you can do it that way. Many of my friends follow the spectator's path and that seems to work for them. They get just a tiny fragment here and there. To get a larger sense of a peak moment, I find that I myself, must be engaged; not just a spectator. But each of us has to find our own path."

The remainder of the trip followed a predictable course. We completed our new route and met the pickup truck at the appointed hour at Moose Lake. Back in Ely, we proceeded in time-honored fashion by having dinner at Vertin's. Dr. Bob found a piano in one of the bars. He was in rare form as he played and sang the entire musical from the Princeton class play of 1923. He had on a tweed jacket, yellow sport shirt buttoned at the neck, tan trousers carefully creased, and a white handkerchief in his breast pocket. It was strange to see him standing at the bar alongside burly iron miners in their wool shirts and billed caps. Yet he had such an amazing presence, he sold his differences as something entertaining and not something to take offense at.

I returned to school feeling like a professional. I had now spent over 200 days in the bush and had paddled a minimum of 2000 miles. I walked down the streets in my clean Levi's, wool socks, moccasins, and wool shirt, feeling like a man. I was beginning to sense that I was going to do something important, and make a difference in people's lives. For the moment, I had no idea how this might come about; it was just that I felt capable of finding my own path.

When I returned to Robinson Lake, I was quietly accepted as a man who worked, and that was good. However, very few of the local guides had strong reputations as family men. Everyone knew there was little money to be made as a commercial canoe guide. As for the long trips to strange lakes, why should anyone go that far when you could catch all the lake trout you needed in Lac La Croix? My path was not something that produced extended family argument or anger, it was just a perturbation that could be ignored. The family knew that eventually I would straighten out; in the meantime, they simply enjoyed the show.

I knew that my father was proud of what I was doing as a guide, even though he never mentioned it outright. Only once did he come close to saying what he felt about it all. It was late on a fall Saturday afternoon, and we had come to town for supplies. This included a careful inspection of several bars as we readied ourselves for the return trip. He stood talking to two iron miners about the sacred trilogy: hunting, fishing, and the weather. I was leaning against the bar, only half listening, when he suddenly reached down, grabbed my left boot by the heel, and levered it with both hands up on the bar, "Look at the goddamn muscle in that boot. The kid has been out in the bush all summer. Works as a canoe guide for Bill Rom." They stared at the leg on the bar. Being old friends, they nodded politely. Then the conversation drifted off onto the pros and cons of Bill Rom's outfitting company versus the two older canoe companies. No one asked the opinion of the newly licensed guide standing with one boot on the bar. Although a young man of promise, I lacked the experience for a full involvement in the affairs of men.

The ritual of the fall caught us up in the sequence of wood making, fall trout fishing, deer hunting, waiting in blinds for incoming northern flights of bluebills, then making ice, and waiting for Christmas. The bush was now far away. Sometimes Bob Olson and I would talk about going further north to Hudson's Bay. Only one man in Ely had ever been there. The local knowledge had it that such a trip could be very dangerous, with hundreds of miles of white water rapids and big open water. We knew that the idea was just adolescent fantasy, though. Besides, the war clouds loomed on the near horizon and it seemed likely that all of us would soon become involved. This was not a time for long-range plans.

5

War

By 1943, the fingers of war had touched the family. Uncle Buster and Junior were both in the armed forces. Junior had disappeared after the fall of Corregidor. We heard finally that he was in a Japanese prison camp. But to those of us still in the village at Robinson Lake, all of that seemed very distant. It was deep winter, and Grandma still made her daily rounds to each outpost manned by a daughter or daughter-in-law. Wearing a huge scarf looped around her shoulders and neck and a black cloth coat down to her ankles, she moved with a walking stick in one hand and shopping bag in the other. She was nature's implacable force, moving in a protective circle around the family. Nose red from the cold, she would announce her arrival by shaking the outside door free of snow, then burst in the house: "Hie! Hie! Morgan." It was the same ritual each day, at each house. A quiet check on the course of yesterday's sore throat. Did Hugo finally come home last night? Do you have enough wood? Do you need anything from town? Yesterday's threads would be gathered up and woven into today's events to make the fabric of caring and concern that defined the family.

The Ely public schools were supported by taxes from the deep shaft mines producing quantities of iron ore for the war effort. The resulting taxes produced a cadre of excellent teachers and a first-rate education. My history teacher, Mrs. Paulson, started me on a course of reading that included Upton Sinclair, literature on the American labor movements, and anti-trust legislation. I had a vague sense that changes were needed, but no clear sense that I should be involved. I moved with a small circle of Bob Olson's friends, Harlan Lampi, and Bud Larson. We had no clear sense of purpose or direction other than we were the talented good guys that would one day ferret out injustice and serve as attack dogs in unnamed good causes. I made vague plans to attend the local junior college. Sig Olson, my boss at the Border Lakes Outfitters, was also the dean of the college. This seemed like a promising bridge to the future.

Our class had only a few hundred students so it was possible to explore almost any activity that was of interest. I made random selections ranging from the drama club to the school newspaper, swimming team, and the Latin club. Although occasionally on the honor roll, I was not an outstanding student. I had no particular motivation to compete for high grades. Other than the swimming team, I did not really sample the world of competition; and even there, I lacked the fierce desire to win that characterized real champions.

I was seduced by a glib speech teacher into my one other effort to compete—joining the statewide extemporaneous speaking contest. Each participant spent months reading in depth, covering an extensive sampling of *Reader's Digest* type articles on foreign policy. I did surprisingly well in the regional contests. I represented Ely attired in the brown suit I had bought for my confirmation ceremony several years earlier. The cuff of the jacket only came part way down my arms; I liked to think it gave me a Lincolnesque quality.

For the state meet, Mrs. Freer and I drove all the way to Duluth. She was as nervous as I was, but more about the complicated traffic than the contest itself. I was sitting in the middle of the auditorium when the speaker announced, "And now, Jerry Patterson from Ely will speak on Swedish Foreign Policies in the 1940s." I was elated because I had extensively prepared for this particular topic. As I stood up, I heard the unique sound of overwrought fabric giving way. As far as I could tell, standing before an audience of several hundred, the seat of my pants had been ripped asunder from belt loop to fly. I walked to the stage wondering if my jacket covered the exposure. I was flooded with tiny questions about the status of the particular underwear I had put on that morning. My focus kept shifting from Sweden's present difficulties to my own desperate situation. I gave a sorry performance, thus ending my first effort to become a serious competitor.

Ms. Freer, my speech teacher, had graduated from an Ivy League school. It seemed that I and Ely's other graduates simply did not measure up to her high standards in that we could not compare to the elite student body encountered in east coast prep schools. Later that spring when congratulating me on winning the year's Rotary Club Award for scholarship and citizenship, she added this friendly warning: "Gerald, you may have a certain amount of talent. But be careful that you do not set your sights too high."

I became swept up in a very active social life, but one that did not, at first, include attendance at school dances. Aunt Fanny and her dour following of Senior Lutherans forbad dancing as a sinful activity. Although the Robinson Lake adults did not share these views, each child decided on their course of action. One evening in my junior year, three of my buddies actually burst through the door, wrestled me to the floor, and tied me with ropes. My astonished mother was told that they were simply taking me to my first dancing lesson. They carried me out onto the dance floor, untied me, and turned me over to Lois Maki, one of the school's more attractive and better dancers. Perhaps in recognition of that late start, that year I was elected Homecoming King. It was a beautiful fall evening with all the lights in the football stadium turned on. It was half time. The Homecoming Queen, with her silver tiara, sat with me in the back of a red convertible. We waved in regal fashion up to the stands of clapping and cheering people. The experience did not fit into anything that had ever happened to me before. The picture kept slipping in and out of focus. Suddenly, there was a jagged outburst from one end of the stands, and I spotted a wedge of uncles, burly figures waving bottles and shouting, "Jer! JERRRYYYY!" My father was shouting, "That's my son!" We never discussed the incident. There was no need to; they had let me know as dramatically as they could that they were proud.

Years later, I was speechless when an old acquaintance explained to a group of new friends that this event proved that I had emerged from a disadvantaged family. All the way through school, I had felt that my family was an elite force, and that other families simply could not measure up. All the men in my family measured up to my standard of what a man should be. They all worked and took care of their families. Each one of them had a special set of skills. As a group, they knew how to survive in the wilderness. Fathers and uncles who owned grocery stores or managed transport companies simply could not hold a candle to the colorful males who formed my family. I liked the fact that they were unconventional.

More than a half century later, when I brought a grandson home to meet the family, I loved the incredulous expression on his face when people explained to him that his great-grandfather used to go into bars and slip live minnows in people's beers just to start some excitement. It was my incredible good fortune to be brought up in such good company.

At midsummer I was drafted into the U.S. Army. Twelve draftees left Ely on a late summer morning in a Greyhound bus bound for Fort Snelling, Minneapolis. There were no philosophical discussions on the bus, but I think most of us felt that we were embarking upon a just cause. I approached the situation with a deep sense of pride and personal worth. I was convinced that like my Uncle Junior in the marines, I would do more than my share of whatever needed to be done. Like a lot of young men, I knew privately that my parents' concern for my safety was groundless. I knew that nothing could happen to me.

The train was taking us to Fort Hood, Texas. Four of us were in the kitchen car with the door open, seated around a tub peeling potatoes. I knew I had seen this movie before, but this time I was in the film, watching the train lean into the corner with its ends out of sight. The kitchen squad was also like a cast from a Hollywood war movie. There was one little guy from New York with an unbelievable dialect and cynical street lingo, two others from Appalachia, and I, myself, from Minnesota.

Through the open door we could see the hot, flat country sliding by. The roads edged off to the horizon like grid lines, and an unfriendly August sun turned the country into dust and haze. It was a man-made world of hot little squares and rectangles. Even the trees were planted in straight lines. This was farm country. To me it was a strange, unfriendly country; a place where nature had lost its battle with man. I felt I could not survive here. The water that I could occasionally see looked stagnant. I could see no places inviting me to pitch a tent and stay the night. This land was owned. It was barricaded with little fences so nothing could freely move from one square to another.

The train took us all to a new world: Fort Hood, Texas, one of those places that seemed like a divine experiment to determine what happens when you place an area too close to a blazing, angry sun. Even at night, the leftover heat stayed with you. During the day, standing in formation, the sun was always in close attendance. It was a narrow world of flags, John Phillip Sousa's music, and a constant trickle of sweat running down the back. Basic training was actually interesting to me as in a way, the training by the family had been tailored-made to produce soldiers. Cooperation quickly translated to obedience. Our love of guns, shooting, and basic survival were perfect preparation for basic training in the infantry. The infantry meant good food and all you could eat. It meant guns, with a lot of shooting. It meant carrying packs that were much lighter than anything we used in the Quetico. I was confident that I could master whatever they had to teach.

113

However, if there was one feature of military life that I found difficult, it was the emphasis upon blind obedience to direct commands. Issuing direct commands was simply not done in Robinson Lake. Accompanying a command with a curse was unheard of. One day, Staff Sergeant McKearn, an unremarkable figure with a slightly sagging middle and a soft, but perpetually red face, stood in the center of the squad, hands on hips, screaming "Goddammit, I want these pieces clean!" Then a shouted, "Understand?" as he wheeled, glowering at each of us in turn. Dramatic as it was, it didn't come off very well because his voice was thin and tended to break at just the wrong moment. As instructed, each of us had begun working on the barrel and breach of a BAR rifle lying on a poncho beside us. This was at the end of a long day on the firing range, and there was very little talking. First we had to apply a clean patch and then solvent and a wire brush to work out today's accumulation in the rifling. Clean patch, then solvent, and another clean patch, until the bore was a gleaming stainless steel tunnel, absolutely spotless. When I was finished, I stood up and walked it over to where the sergeant stood talking to the platoon leader. As I handed it to him, he managed a scowl and held the barrel up in the air, squinting into it. "What the hell you doing, Patterson? I told you to clean this piece. Look at this!" He flicked an imaginary piece of lint from the chamber, then thrust the barrel at me as he howled over my shoulder to the squad, "I said clean. I mean fucking clean. Now jump to it." I was stunned. I knew the barrel was clean. The sergeant knew it was clean. So what was the shouting about? Marching, shooting, running obstacle courses, everything had a game-like quality to it, almost like still being in high school. I could build a bridge from Robinson Lake to all of the other army experiences, but not to this one. I stood in shock for several seconds, clutching the rifle barrel, mouth open and speechless. My white-faced rage registered on both of us. He stepped back. I had no idea what to do. I wanted to hit him. As I turned away, he growled, "And clean it right this time, goddamn."

A fellow recruit named Sid looked up as I walked stiff-legged back into our circle, "Hey, Minnesota, what's chewing on you?" Sid was the old man in our unit. A former social studies teacher, he was married and in his late twenties. A Mexican from a large West Coast city, he treated the entire Fort Hood experience as being unreal and downright ridiculous. "Damn it, Sid, look at this rifle. It is clean. The son bitch yelled at me." He stared at me for a moment, took a puff from his cigarette, and laughed, "Shit, kid, no one never yelled at you before?"

I shook my head, "Hell no, not like that. At home you don't talk that way to a man unless you're getting ready to fight." He bent over his rifle barrel, sides shaking with laughter. Then looking past me, "Where in hell you think you are, man? You don't dig this place at all!" I held my head down. I didn't want the group to see how much McKearn had gotten to me, "Fucking officers. I'll do what I'm asked. I don't need some son of a bitch yelling at me to do something." Sid was bent over his rifle barrel, running a dry patch and checking the barrel.

"Yeah, Minnesota, maybe you would, coming out of the north woods and all. But I tell you one thing, kid; the rest of us wouldn't. Want something done, you let 'em know you mean it. Yell. Scare the shit out of em." It was not clear whether he was talking to me or to himself. Sid sat with his sides still shaking, and in an imitation of my voice, "He yelled at me." He did not look up and did not stop working on the rifle. "What do you mean, you don't talk to a man that way? What makes you think you're a fucking man here, in this place? You dumb shit." He laughed softly to himself, "Hey, north woods man, this was all worked out before you came along, and before Sergeant McKearn came along, or anybody else here. This is a game, man. In this game you are a digit. It was a Frenchman, Michel Le Tellier, in about 1650 who set this up. What the cat learned was that if you take a bunch of guys and put them on the drill field doing close order formations, a funny thing happens."

Half the squad was now sitting in the hot sun listening to Sidello talk to himself as he oiled each piece before slipping it in place. Henny sat next to him, thin shoulders bent forward in a perpetual bow, balding, looking more like forty than twenty. He had spent his life traveling with a carnival. "Sheeeit, you talking as if you know about this cat," Henny said. "If you are so goddamn smart, why aren't you a fucking officer?" Sid shifted the cigarette to the center of his mouth.

"University of Chicago graduate school in political science. And not everyone wants to be an officer. Asshole."

Some of the rage had subsided and I knew I could talk now. "So what has this old guy got to do with McKearn, and this screwed up game?"

Sid nodded his head. "You get a bunch of guys practicing taking orders all day from their officer, what do you think happens?" Sid turned and looked directly at me as he asked the question. There was an edge to his voice now that hadn't been there a minute ago. "When it's killing time, that same officer is giving commands you've been conditioned to obey. You do what he says even if you and your buddies are getting the shit blown out of you. McKearn was just reminding you that is what it's all about. The whole thing is to get you to do what the officers tell you to do, even if it means getting your ass blown off. We're not talking about men, kid; we're talking about little robots. Now tell me about being a man, kid. A man, in this fucked up place."

My face was flushed and my voice uncertain. "I don't need someone to tell me when to shoot," I said. I knew I had lost the argument and couldn't think of anything else to say. Sid sat staring off into space. He reminded me of Joe Chosa with his broad face and flattened cheekbones, but with a lot more to say. His voice was low, sad, and insistent. "They worked all this out in their European wars two hundred years ago," he said. "The most efficient killing gets done when you have officers to give orders and men trained on drill fields to do what they're told. Killing is what it's about.

Killing." He shook his head as if to clear it, sighed, and went back to putting the BAR together. "Being a man has nothing to do with it."

For the most part, we were taught by sergeants and lieutenants in small groups. Each skill was presented as having life-saving potential. It was implied that being dead meant you had probably screwed up in some way. In an abstract sense, combat was presented as if it were high school football. If you were well trained and did what you were supposed to do, you would make it. We were told that we were the best trained and best equipped soldiers in the world (neither of which was true). Dying was like losing the game. Each week we learned new ways to survive, new skills. Weaving shuttle-like through all these activities were the activities of the drill field. The radio, letters from home, all worked to make this seem like a short-term make-believe canoe trip from which we would soon come home. We were shown movies that emphasized the fact that the enemy were bad people and deserved to die. We learned from the chaplain that God was on our side. Each day's experience normalized the day before it, and the day yet to come. Each day was a step taking each of us away from our individual Robinson Lakes.

Most of us were adolescents and most of us strongly believed in the training we received. Those of us with extra energy would practice the skills in the evening: the rifle drills, the hand-to-hand judo holds, and boxing. Each barracks had several sets of boxing gloves. On weekends groups would gather between the barracks. The gloves and challenges would travel around the circle of bodies that formed the rings. One Saturday afternoon, a soldier named Henny was coming back from town carrying a full load of beer. The way Henny's body was put together suggested a kind of odds-and-ends approach. He was short-waisted, with arms that were too long and hands that were much too big. His clothes just didn't hang right, he looked rumpled no matter what he had on. He stood beside me now in full costume, with his tie off, hat covering

117

only the back of the head. He gave us a big grin as he pressed his bag of beer up against my sweaty shirt. "Hey, Minnesota here says he can whip any motherfucker from east of the Mississippi." A loud cackle could be heard as he shouted that phrase several times. Heads swiveled in my direction, one man took the challenge and I was quickly launched in a new career.

Henny put his sack down as he tied gloves on my sweaty hands. He looked over at the large, somewhat overweight figure also having his gloves laced on. "Ever box, kid?" he asked me. I shook my head. "Naw, not much." He turned me away from the ring for a second and said, "Look, I used to train carnie boxers. Lead with a long left; out here like this." Henny moved well. His figure quickly changed from old man with an emphysema chest and too-long arms, to a fighter propelled by fluid, balanced motion.

A rebel yell from behind me announced that the bout was beginning. My opponent launched his first punch. His glove was a huge balloon that seemed to float very slowly. I picked up his punch with my left glove and countered with a right to his head. The punch surprised us all. Henny yelled, "Two beers on Minnesota. We got one here." My opponent was so unnerved by that sudden exchange that he moved away from any efforts to further engage. I was too surprised to follow up.

These bouts seldom lasted more than a few minutes. My opponent made no objections when another champion from the Deep South was shoved forward by friends. Henny grinned and sucked his can dry. "Trapper Jack, I'll bet you don't even know what in hell a counterpunch is, do you?" I was stripped down to my undershirt and dripping sweat and confusion. I did not really want to go on with this. But on the other hand, I could not see how to get out of the situation honorably. "Look, kid, I think you got fast hands. Just keep working the left. Jab with it. Move it. Okay?"

I had a trainer. Henny kept me in the circle for another three bouts, then picked up his sack and walked me back to the barracks.

Each night thereafter, Henny and I cleared a space up on the second floor of the barracks and he would work with me. "Come on, you big dumb Norwegian, watch my motherfucking left hand." His hands moved with amazing speed, flicking my nose, and forehead almost at will. "Shit, kid, every time you use your left, you drop your right. You act like you wanna get your head knocked off." After a few weeks, most everyone would want to spar with me or with Henny, and our hot, sweaty Texas nights were filled with young men pretending to be Joe Louis.

After several months of training, Henny moved the experience to its next stage. He talked to the CO about putting me up as a candidate for company boxer. He asked for released time so we could train. I could have said no, but again I could think of no way of backing out of the situation, which was rapidly getting out of control. I went over to the gym and watched boxers working out. It was not reassuring. These men moved like pros. They definitely did not drop their right guard when they threw a left jab. I was outclassed, and I knew it.

Still, I enjoyed the game-like quality of our evening and weekend sessions in the barracks. A dozen of us had the space cleared and were taking turns late one Saturday night. We heard the front door slam and Sgt. McKearn's voice growling downstairs, "Who the hell is here? Who? Oh, shit, those candy-assed kids playing boxer with that goddamn Henny? Not one of them can punch their way out of wet Kleenex." He heaved himself up the stairs and stood in the doorway with his drinking buddy, glaring at us. I had the gloves on. No one was saying anything. "So this is the kid from Minnesota. Hear you're a dancer. Like these other shitheads, you never really been in a fight, have you?" His small red eyes were squinting at me as he spoke. "Have you?" I shrugged. I felt angry and frightened at the same time. I could feel what was coming. I wanted it to happen. I could feel my heart start to pound.

"Well, I have been, hear? Gimme those fucking gloves.

119

Patterson and me gonna do some fancy training." He took off his tie, hat, and shirt, and stood in the circle of light getting his gloves laced on. We were about the same height and weight. He carried his hands low as he circled. Suddenly he leaped forward, swinging both hands at once in a rapid flurry. I caught one roundhouse with my glove, but his simultaneous blow from the left caught me on the side of the head. Before I could get my guard up, he caught me twice more in the same flurry. This was an assault, a barroom brawl. It made our make-believe boxing sessions "goddamn kids' games," just like McKearn had said.

"Hold still, Patterson. I'm going to teach you fighting. Fuck this boxing." The blows he landed were delivered too quickly. They were more like slaps than punches. They distracted me, but they did not actually hurt that much. In between flurries he was taking my repeated jabs on his unprotected mouth and nose. During each of his attacks, his blood-smeared face would contort just before he lunged. There would be quick flurry of blows on my gloves, shoulders, and arms. Yet each attack cost him. Finally, he said, "Aw, shit, got enough, kid?" and without looking at me, he turned and walked away. The gloves were still tied on his hands.

For a few days in our make-believe world, I was a hero. After my seminar with Sgt. McKearn, I thought that maybe I had a future as a boxer after all. But it was at this point that I received my first real boxing lesson, delivered by a very unlikely teacher. His name was Pesak, and he was huge, but he was quiet. He stood on the edges of things, always looking interested, but not joining in. He liked to stand at the back of the group when we were boxing, and he could never be enticed to put on the gloves.

It was a hot Sunday afternoon. I was laying on my bunk writing letters when Pesak came up to me. "Hey, Jer, wanna box?" he asked. In my newfound status as hero, I could refuse no such request. All challenges had to be met. My support section was nowhere in sight as we walked out of the barrack's shadow and into a square of bright sunlight. Each of us silently laced our own gloves and slipped our hands into them. Pesak stood in one place. I circled about him jabbing and weaving. Every once in a while he would throw a great howitzer of a punch that moved the air like some great fan. He never even got close to me as I danced about him, flicking a left on his head and sometimes his face.

It was very hot out and each time I moved, my boots made scraping his sounds and raised little clouds of dust. Pesak stood, gloves up in front of his face, bent over with his shoulders hunched over his head like some giant musk ox. Nobody was cheering, nobody watching, nobody caring. This did not fit the make-believe boxing world that I was familiar with. The bout was going on much too long. There were no rules about how to stop or even how to end a round. So we both shuffled around, panting and punching. Then from out of nowhere, stars appeared all around me. There were dazzling lights and then pain. Pesak had landed a punch. For me, the make-believe world totally stopped at this point. We hunched about, both bleeding from the nose, flint eyes watching each other carefully behind our glove barricades. The pain was incredible, never in all the make-believe boxing had anyone connected such a blow. Now we both settled down to the serious business of hurting each other. Punches came more slowly; we were each breathing hard. Finally we both stood motionless. I dropped my hands, "Ah, what the hell, Pesak, how about a beer at the PX?" He nodded his head. We touched gloved hands as we walked toward the stairs. My boxing lesson was over.

Pesak and I never did become friends, nor did either of us ever mention the exchange. But that day barrack boxing lost its fascination for me. Henny never understood how could I possibly turn down a career as a carnie boxer. He often came by with his brown paper sack. "Christ, kid, you could be great," he said. "With hands like that we could travel all around the country." He always forgot to tell me about the pain.

I had gone home that Christmas in my army uniform with the usual medal, each of its four bars attesting to the skills I now had.

121

As a trained combat soldier, I believed that if I were skilled enough with these weapons, everything would be all right. My mother and father did not believe this, but there was no way that they could say it. I was on a carousel that they could not control, and that carousel was taking me far away from Robinson Lake. Instead, we talked of the coming deer season. Even though I was the honored guest, it was clear that I was no longer walking the path of the family. I was going somewhere else.

The train was moving north, up the coast toward a replacement depot outside of Seattle. In the early morning's half-light I could just make out huge tall shapes in the mist. The wheel clicks were so slow I wondered whether we were moving at all. We were actually going over the top of a pass and down the western slope of the Washington Cascades. There were austere, dark colors everywhere, and strange black rock cliffs with the windblown mist moving through fringes of trees. There were no man-made structures in sight. Untracked white snow stretched around and behind blue and black trunk columns. These huge trees had only a few branches on their lower reaches—otherwise they stood clean and naked. Their tops interlocked to form a dark roof over black trunks and white snow. Each trunk was drawn in straight lines. A tree leaning, or one with a curve to it, was noticeably out of place. Here and there, a small stream came straight down a rock face to disappear under the tracks. I saw two places where tents could be put up. I mentally put on my Duluth pack and snow shoes to follow some of the ridges that swept out in long lines radiating from the tracks, only to disappear below into the fog. I had never seen mountains before. I knew as I sat with my face pressed against the window that I had found my place, my center. The train full of sleeping soldiers moved down the pass. There was one face attending.

The troop ship was a marvel of interconnectedness. Everything was orderly. Space and time were carefully planned so that there were no loose ends. The ship had to accommodate thousands of men sleeping eighteen inches from each other. We lined up for everything from candy bars to saltwater showers. Only the ocean itself could disrupt such order. As we left the port of Seattle, the wind moved heavily across the water, stirring up huge waves. The ship was in convoy and blacked out. Dim red lights lit the halls and heavy double layers of canvas covered all hatchways. The latrines, of course, were full of sick men. We lined up for the mess hall. Inside, with each rolling wave, the trays slid down the long tables we stood against. As regular as a commuter train, the line of trays would come clacking by, bringing both yours and your neighbor's unfinished supper. The neighbor had often left long ago to be sick. Eventually the trays shot out over the floor to greet the next group as they came in.

At each replacement depot—first in Hawaii then in Saipan—there was more training, more marching, and more shooting. We began practicing loading and unloading from ships. In Saipan, we went on long patrols searching for the few Japanese who remained hidden in caves in the jungle. We became more proficient. We absorbed the implicit doctrine that only fuck-ups die and shipped out once more to an unknown destination. Each day on shipboard there would be formations to stand, group exercises, and small teaching groups. But these intrusions by officers were brief. For me, life centered primarily on four or five buddies with whom I spent the day reading books, playing poker, or caught up in the moment-by-moment experience of a combat ship. We spent little time thinking about the big picture. The smell of diesel oil from the engines, the gray painted anti-aircraft guns, and the ships and destroyers stretching to the far horizon, all made for a sense of excitement and purpose. Each time we approached the low black silhouette of an island on the horizon, the excitement would mount.

The silhouette of Okinawa in April of 1945 looked like any other island. The actual invasion had occurred a week or two earlier. We came in on landing craft and waded up onto a beach in the darkness. On the beaches, there were no signs of combat that you could see. We were replacements walking south to catch up with the 7th Division, 184th Regiment, F Company. When we arrived, they had just been pulled off the firing line at Yonabaru. The fifty or so replacements, including myself, were lined up without dispatch and rank ordered from tallest to shortest. Taller, bigger men were assigned to weapons squads, where size would count to good advantage in carrying heavy weapons and mortar shells.

I was assigned to the mortar squad, which had three other members: Sergeant "Bloody," Guido, and Charley. All of them had started with the Division during the fighting in Alaska, then the Philippines, and now here. Guido was an older but less educated version of Sidello. He had worked with horses in New Mexico. He was a big, slow moving, and slow talking Mexican. I was assigned to his tent. Nothing was said about the man I replaced, who they had lost earlier in the week. The next few days were taken up with practice sessions, setting up the mortar, repairing equipment, writing letters, and standing guard. The Japanese infiltrated the lines each night. Their progress could be marked by sudden fire fights, with tracers making their strange, slow moving paths across a black sky.

We walked single file in a winter-cold drizzle through one small valley after another. We were now up on a ridge and could see in the distance the huge brown mass that was Mt. Shun. It was the center of the Japanese line. On the other side of the dirt road a single file of troops was moving to the rear. These were the people we were to replace. As they left their foxholes, our lines filed into them. The exchange took only a few minutes, and soon Guido and I were in a foxhole high up on a ridge overlooking the tiny village of Yonabaru. We seemed to be the last foxhole on the east end of the line. We could see big ships far out at sea. I pointed at the ships. "Damn why didn't I sign up to be sailor? Lucky bastards sleep in warm bunks and get warm food every night."

Guido shook his head and said very quietly, "Naw, you don't mean that kid. Wait till you see a couple kamikaze planes diving on those poor guys. Not so lucky." Guido said very little, but when he did, it was real quiet and polite.

Every twenty feet or so, there was another hole with one or two men in it. Our mortar was behind us, down in a hollow right next to an Okinawan tomb. The village was immediately below us. To our front, a few hundred yards away, there was a small cluster of thatched roof farm buildings, surrounded by a stone fence. The hill we were on stretched far off, climbing to the right. At about midpoint, it was bisected by a ridge that flowed up from the valley floor below. There were small clumps of pine trees separating ridge from valley floor. A mile beyond that there was a tiny patchwork of fields and small creek beds, and behind it and surmounting it all was Mt. Shuri. Its massive pyramid shape was shaded blue-black when the storms swept in, and light tan and gray when the sun appeared. The Japanese had huge gun ports carved into the mountain itself.

On the evening of May 3rd, every available gun on the Japanese Shuri line opened fire. The barrage was meant to soften up our defenses in preparation for a major frontal attack. High above our heads the air was filled with murmuring voices, first from one direction and then answered from the other. Up on the mountain they periodically rolled out a huge Bertha of a gun. They would fire it and then quickly trundle it back into the mountain before our counter-batteries could find it. The shell from the big gun traveled a great looping trajectory high above us, and then dropped at an acute angle. It sounded like a freight car looping end over end. Then, directly above us, the sound would stop. Seconds later a great gout of sound and earth would rise up on our ridge.

The earth shook and heaved all about us as Guido and I tried to sink through the bottom of our foxhole. Far away, men were screaming; voices called insistently for "Medic!" Neither Guido or I spoke to the other. There was nothing to say that made any sense. I knew for certain that the screams came from men no less skilled than I. This was the end-point of the game. Each step to-

125

ward it had been simple, clear, and game-like in quality, but now, you could hear the dying and the maiming all around you, and you knew it was entirely random.

If a shell struck our foxhole, it would be entirely by chance. Each shell that came in had its own sound, whispering and demanding that you listen because maybe this message could be a personal one. I knew nauseating fear for the first time, the way it fills up your throat. There was a sense of everything being sped up and out of control. I had to find some way of stepping outside of it all.

"What the hell you doing, kid?"

"Shakespeare," I shouted, and Guido laughed and put his head down between his knees again. "Why not?" I forced myself to say the words. I was not reading, just saying words. Inside of the cover there were the pictures of Jeanne. Focus on beautiful blonde girl sitting in a canoe. More screams from up on the ridge. Look at the picture. Read the words. Don't listen; don't think. Hold the picture.

The shelling continued off and on through the night, and then at dawn, finally, it stopped. Guido's stocky frame was half out of the foxhole. "Jesus, what is that?" Far out in the cane field, a column of flame shot up. Tiny figures literally danced about it. Sergeant Bloody in the next foxhole held the binoculars steady for a moment. "Those are Jap soldiers. They fired up those two tanks of ours that got it yesterday. Hey, lieutenant, get some artillery over there! Where the hell are our guys?"

In the early morning light, they came in columns headed by flag bearers. Out there in the gloom, the Japanese 89th Regiment was moving toward us. They were heading up the tongue that projected perpendicularly from our ridge. They were a thousand yards away when the column split. Half of them were coming around toward the village that lay immediately below us. They were moving at a run and quickly disappeared behind a grove of trees. The other column continued to move toward the center of our line. I could

126

see their officers off to the side, running along holding their swords. The flags were waving as if it were some slow-motion film. They were shouting and blowing bugles. You could hear them now. I could see some of our soldiers getting out of their fox-holes and running. Our officers were shouting commands and some had taken their carbines by the barrel and were clubbing men back into their holes.

From behind us, Bloody came running up, low to the ground. "Guido, you and the kid stay up here. We'll work the mortar from right behind you. Take this; I picked it up yesterday when some-body got careless and left it in their jeep." It was a scope-mounted Springfield '06, a sniper's rifle. Guido handed it to me, "Kid, you any good with one of those? I've got the binoculars . . . get you ze-roed in." I took the rifle, set the sling, and lay on the ground in front of our foxhole. Even with the scope, the targets were still tiny figures. I set for maximum range and began to fire. "Naw, can't see where you are hitting, keep firing." Another clip. "Hey, kid, I saw it. You're left a couple feet and short." Another clip. "That's it, kid. One of 'em is down."

The scope picked up running figures appearing then disap-pearing in the smoke. I tried to focus on one figure at a time. Then I'd fire. Where was the column that was moving toward us? They were still out of sight. I tried to stay focused on the group moving to the center. I was sweating and could feel the heat of the gun as I focused the scope again. The field was shrouded in smoke or fog, and the figures did not stand still. I fired. They were closer now. Sometimes I could see when I connected and the figure fell. I'd put in another clip and pull back the bolt, experiencing strange distant thoughts from far away. The feel of my own 30 '06, now thou-sands of miles away, and the flicker of a deer running up a snowy ridge. Fire. Load. I was thirsty. Why did they keep coming? I fo-cused on the solder with a pack carrying barbed wire. Fire. What the hell was he doing with that?

Suddenly puffs of dirt a foot high marched up the hill right over our foxhole. I didn't see where the machine gun fire came from. Now there was a Japanese soldier right below us, coming up the hill two hundred yards away. Suddenly the area below us was filled with running figures. Guido was firing now, too. "Get in the hole, kid. Use the M-1." I could hear our mortar shells pouring into the section of the village right in front of us. Our artillery was zeroed in on the column moving up the ridge to our right. Through the smoke I could see two figures right in front of us, running bent over, carrying a heavy machine gun on a kind of litter. Now there was sporadic fire coming directly at us. I still couldn't see where it was coming from. It was impossible to organize the welter of sounds and images into a coherent picture; we simply fired at anything that moved. On the ground, bodies were strewn in random patterns. My God! Here came a group carrying strange pieces of heavy equipment as if they meant to set up housekeeping. For Christ's sake, was anyone else there? There was no pleasure in seeing someone fall. It was not possible to keep any kind of score. At most, I merely had a sense of doing my job. Everything seemed disconnected.

Periodically, I ran back a few hundred feet to the supply dump and looped as many bandoleers of rifle ammunition as I could over my shoulder. Then I'd run back to the foxhole feeling very exposed. There was no big picture, just a jumble of disconnected slides with no theme tying them together. There was no sense of time. Artillery fire slowed down and stopped. There were still brief spurts of movement and firing. The smoke gave all of this a disconnected feeling, and a sense that things had no beginning or ending. There were just little pieces of something. Most of the time it was impossible to tell if you had hit anything unless . . . , they, were right in front of you. Our position was at the end of the ridge; for some reason, none of the running figures had tried to get around to our left.

The firing had slowed; it felt as if the tide was ebbing. There were no longer any massed figures running at the position through the smoke. The heavy artillery stopped, and eventually the mortars as well. Over the course of the day, Guido and I had fired twenty-three bandoliers. The forearm of my rifle was bleached to an off color. The barrel was too hot to touch. It did not feel like a victory, and there was no celebration. The attack was over. It had failed. I suddenly felt very tired.

Late that afternoon, a small group of Japanese soldiers did try to work around to our left. For some reason, they were moving out in the open where they could be seen. Guido and I fired at them and two of them dropped. The others disappeared. A blanket of motor shells failed to flush them out. The next morning a group from our platoon was assigned to check out our immediate front. It was reported there were still some Japanese soldiers in the area. We filed down into the village, feeling exposed; easy targets. No one fired at us as we spread out in pairs into the village. Guido and I went through the stone gate one at a time. Guido motioned me toward the front door and waved himself around the back. I stood at the edge of the doorway, heart pounding in my ears as I tried to listen to what might be inside. I moved quickly through the door, with my rifle pointing first at one dark corner and then another. I heard a soft rustle of cloth behind me and pivoted desperately to shoot. For some reason, I did not pull the trigger. I hesitated; I could not clearly see what was there. As I walked closer, I could see it was a frail old woman cowering in the corner. The sleeve of her kimono had slid to her shoulder; I could see blue tattoo marks covering her entire arm. Her face was contorted with fear, eyes very round. I slung my rifle on my shoulder and spoke gently as I knelt beside her. As I reached to pick her up, she moved farther into the corner. I sat on my heels for a moment, speaking softly to her and then reached out again, smiling as I did so and pointing to the door. She allowed me to pick her up. I walked past Guido standing in the courtyard. "Take her to the Aid Station, kid." He smiled as he saw the tattoos. "Bet she has an interesting story to tell. Could have been a high-class geisha lady." I walked back up the hill carrying this tiny woman and felt like a hero, a real hero. I was terribly pleased that I had not pulled the trigger.

Each day, there were further patrols. A group from our company was assigned to check the other side of the hill that bisected our ridge. I asked to join. Guido was standing watching and came up behind me, "Kid, don't be stupid. Never volunteer for anything, especially for a fucking patrol. You can get your ass shot off out there." I put my head down and walked away without answering. I still viewed the war game through a boy's eyes. I am not sure, but I think I felt I could protect the others.

The patrol moved along our position, past the bisecting ridge and down its far side. We moved single file toward a small field that was traversed by a low stone wall. We moved along the stone wall, grateful for even that small measure of comfort. The Japanese dead lay in what seemed an orderly formation. It seemed like an entire company laid out side by side in rows. It looked as if the entire mass had charged into an interlocking field of machine gun fire and died in formation. I could see no indication of small groups trying to break away and follow their own course. I had no previous experience with death, yet here was death on a large scale. But it seemed far away. There was no grieving for the dead, theirs or ours.

We spread out and walked slowly through the field. What was in the field had only to do with soldiering. The dead looked as if they might be asleep. They did not fit into any part of my ordinary experience. Other than the sense of relief that it was not me and my squad that lay on that field, all other feelings were locked away.

We dropped all the way down the bisecting ridge to the little cluster of tanks that had pinpointed the start of the attack. There were clutches of bodies here and there where the artillery fire that had found them. We encountered no Japanese patrols. The fields belonged entirely to us.

Within a few days, we had left the ridge and passed through

the village at dawn. For some reason we had been instructed to fix bayonets and proceed through the village without a round in the chamber. It seemed pointless. Now I was afraid, whereas yesterday, my fear had been relatively limited. This felt like a return to ancient forms of conflict: each of us walking along, listening for the telltale sound of a boot moving on the cobblestone. We crossed the valley without incident and started circling the east side of Mt. Shuri. That evening, in the rain, we dug our foxholes up in the foothills overlooking the level ground that we had just crossed. I had been on guard and had just lain down to sleep in the early morning light, when I heard our CO shouting. "There he goes! Get that son of a bitch!" I jumped up. There was a figure dressed in white, loose-fitting pants and shirt running several hundred yards away. I threw my rifle to my shoulder, followed him briefly, and shot. The figure collapsed, and other shots followed. The CO came over to me and said, "That was good shooting, Patterson. The gook was a spy. Good thing you got him." I felt good, until I tried to go back to sleep and Sidello's voice came whispering, "The drill field, kid. He said shoot, and what did you do? Was he really a spy?"

There was no time to reflect about who was responsible. It was no longer clear who was the enemy and who were civilians. There was no sense of anything outside of our group and the immediate moment. There was never enough time to sleep either. Sleep came in small packages, intervals of one hour here or two hours there. I could sleep anywhere. I convinced myself that I actually could go into a light sleep while moving with the column. Sleep could come lying wrapped in a poncho in the bottom of a foxhole that contained several inches of water. Our perpetual lack of sleep hung there like a fog. What was real and not real had become blurred.

We moved farther to the east of Mt. Shuri, now a work detail bringing up supplies to the new line. The column crossed an open field of short-cropped brown winter grass. There were no trees. It looked very much like the open foothills in a Montana mountain range. I was carrying a case of grenades. No one spoke. We were moving through the mud as quickly as we could. We had heard that in this same area, the last supply column had come under heavy shelling that came from the hills off to the left. We rounded a corner to see equipment strewn all over the ground. There was a pair of shoes sitting by the trail; each one had a foot and ankle still inside. Move, move. That couldn't be real. Move. Guido walked ahead of me, carrying a five gallon can of water in a pack frame and a box of small arms ammo in each hand. His big bulky figure bent forward, slowly pulling first one foot then the other from the mud.

"Guido!"

"Yeah, kid, I saw."

It was raining again, and the mist crept down from the hills. I slipped deep into my head, a distant observer of the pain in the shoulders and arms, wondering how many more steps were possible. The mist protected us from artillery, so we were lucky; but it also made it possible for enemy patrols to slip down unnoticed from the ridge. It was not good to speak of it. Besides, it was too hard to talk.

We tricked ourselves into keeping the killing, the maiming, and the dying out of focus. It was basically the squad—your family of five men—that gave you what little balance there was. The high point of the day came when the camp stove was lit to make soup and warm up the squad rations. Then we could talk. The prime rule was that you never spoke about the men who had been wounded or killed, and were now missing from the squad. They never existed. We moved through the experience a tiny island of five, supporting and protecting each other in an environment that was implacable, overwhelming, and unpredictable. We shared a vaguely enunciated myth about our invincibility. We would make it. Most of us, even Bloody and Guido, who had already been through it all, bought into a version of the drill instructor's myth: If you are really skilled, you don't die. When we were pulled out of line for a few days, we practiced a little bit harder than the other squads in setting up the mortar. We took extra care in cleaning our weapons. We took care of each other. The umbrella was even extended to new replacements like me. There was only a sense of an "us," a "them," and the enemy.

Aside from an occasional shelling, it seemed we had temporarily lost contact with the Japanese. The company was spread out at the base of a small, treeless ridge a few hundred feet high. We had placed two machine guns up on top of the grassless slope. Each gun pit had a small circle of foxholes for the support squad. Shortly before dawn, there had been a series of explosions. Then machine gun fire enfiladed the entire company area; it came from our own guns up on the ridge. Most of the men from the support squads were now down in the company area. Bloody had the squad set up the mortar and was already saturating the ridge. Counter-fire from the company quickly built up to a crescendo, and the firing from the ridge stopped. The CO came over and said, "I need three volunteers to go up there and find out what is going on." He was looking at Charley, Guido, and me as he spoke.

Charley moved up on the far left, Guido in the middle, and I about twenty yards to his right. We walked slowly, crouching as low as we possibly could. The sunrise was breaking behind us. I saw a slight movement off to the side and swiveled to shoot. The American crouched in the foxhole with his knees up close to his helmet did not cry out. He made no sign that he had seen me. I glanced over to see that Charley and Guido were nearing the top of the ridge. There was not much grass on top of the ridge, no cover at all. I found a tiny bush a few inches high and lay down behind it.

As I crawled forward, I had an image of McKearn's bloated red face as he conducted the group through house-to-house combat: "Listen, assholes, don't put your head up to look over a wall. Makes a goddamn great target. You're a big round ball sitting up there, waiting to be shot. If you gotta look, then break the silhouette like this." He crossed his arm in front of his face. I did that now as I shoved the barrel of my rifle over the crest and slid behind the bush. The sun was now above the horizon directly behind us and flooded the valley in front of me with light. There was a mass of Japanese only a few hundred feet below me. Evidently, they saw us, too. Both sides began firing at the same moment. The M-1 was lying on the ground; I held and fired it with my right hand. The hold was not solid so the gun jumped around a good bit. I was excited and just fired into the mass of milling figures without picking out a particular target. I couldn't tell whether I hit anyone or not.

The POP that sounded by my right ear was very loud. It sounded as if a gun had been fired close behind me. I rolled over and saw that the underside of my left wrist had turned a bright purple. There was a neat black hole right in the middle of it. I could not accept the fact that I had been shot. Both Charley and Guido had stopped firing. Charley was rolling back down the hill. Guido was slumped where he lay.

I walked down the hill, slipping in and out of focus. I could hear the mortar bursts coming down on the other side of the ridge. Bloody was standing at the bottom, "Medic! Medic! Goddamn it, Medic." I gave him my rifle, tears streaming down my face, "Shit, Bloody, I'm sorry. I got my ass shot off. I . . ." My world was upside down. It could not happen. There was not much pain, but the neat black hole in my wrist destroyed the picture I had of my own invincibility. That split-second event shattered an adolescent bubble that had protected me all this time. I felt that I had somehow fucked up. I was letting my squad down.

"Bloody, there is an attack coming. I fucked up."

"Shut up, you dumb kid. Let me see it. Nice one in the wrist. You get to go home, kid. Let me see the other side." He turned the wrist and hand, "Oh, shit. Where is the fucking morphine? Get over here, assholes. Here it goes. Does it hurt yet, kid? Home," he said. "Go home!"

I was not listening. "Goddammit, Bloody, there were hundreds of them behind that hill. They are getting ready for an attack or something. What the hell you mean, home? I'm staying here. I'll come right back when I get this thing bandaged."

"Naw, kid. You didn't look at the other side of your hand, did ya? You ain't coming back here." He turned and looked back up the hill. More to himself than to anyone, he said, "So, Charley and Guido got it, huh?" I went to my pack and pulled out my handmade combat knife. There were also the two Japanese watches I had taken from the dead officers after the attack on the ridge. I gave these to Bloody. He was embarrassed by the tears. And he could make no sense out of the gifts. He just turned and walked away. I walked around apologizing to whoever would listen. The heroin was beginning to take effect, and the sharp pain in the bandaged hand could now be put out of focus. It existed, but it was far away.

There were people moving up the hill; others were digging in the command post. I could hear the CO calling for artillery support. Charley and Guido were wrapped in ponchos and strapped to stretchers on the back of a weasel. There were two other causalities. We started toward the evacuation area walking under the arching sound of 105 howitzer shells whispering in to drop on the other side of the ridge. All of that seemed far away. As we walked behind the weasel, we could hear the firefight building in intensity. We were walking wounded and we were alive! The pain was far away. The war was far behind us. For the first time, I recaptured the sense of an orderly world, one that I could understand and survive in. We could let ourselves think about home.

As we walked up to the battalion field station, the large pile of arms and legs outside the door of one of the tents was not reassuring. The effects of the drug were wearing off. As I stood in the inevitable line, I was given a glass of wine. I passed out, and awakened as I was being given an anesthetic. Two figures in white gowns were looking at my left hand and arm strapped to the table. One of them was leafing through a book. As I drifted down, I distinctly heard, "Well, what do you think? Should we take it off or not?" It could have been a dream, but it seemed real enough.

I awakened on a cot and saw, or thought I saw, a beautiful woman leaning over me and smiling. I looked down first at the cast on my left hand. I saw fingertips sticking out from the end of the cast, and smiled back. I was all right! I was going home! We were evacuated by plane to the navy hospital at Guam, then after a few weeks by ship to San Francisco. The Letterman hospital was an orderly procession of white sheets, caring staff, and great food. Each of us was assigned to a ward full of patients with similar wounds. The quadriplegics had their own separate ward. I walled that off as effectively as I had the field of the dead in Okinawa.

In the evening, those of us who were presentable could volunteer to be taken by some local sponsoring groups to shows or restaurants in downtown San Francisco. As we entered the restaurant there would be a dead silence as the audience took in the casts, the slings, the crutches and the wheelchairs filing in. People would often stand and clap. Each of us could feel that we were heroes. Now it was possible to feel again. But you could not go back and connect into individual deaths and traumas. They remained locked away for a very long time.

There was a long train ride to a small hospital in Springfield, Missouri. After a series of operations, the consensus was that my left wrist was permanently deflected to a 30-degree angle. The thumb and forefinger were relatively intact but the other three fingers were immobilized, frozen into a claw. I could go home on furlough with the arm in a cast and a full array of combat ribbons. I felt I had been a good soldier. As a nineteen-year-old looks at things, I felt that I was as close to being a hero as ever I would be. We had all participated in a crusade. I also knew with bright clarity that I was no longer immortal. I could die. I could be maimed. The artillery barrages had carried that message.

There were vivid slices from combat locked away in my head, but the feelings about these experiences were gone. I didn't particularly want to talk about them. In fact, when I finally did try, I found that I didn't really have the details clearly in mind. The experiences were a jumble of disconnected slides. There simply was no narrative, no story to tell. I knew from the expression on my family's faces that I was going about it in the wrong way. You could see it in their eyes. Gradually you learned not to speak of it. There was just no way working it in as part of your life. I felt separate from my family, and from life in small-town America. I could see people that I loved leading good lives. That was real enough, most of the time. But those images were now balanced with equally vivid images of killing and maiming. Either view was as real as the other. What most people did not understand was that both images were equally true.

There was, however, one part of me that continued to work on the problem. After my homecoming from the hospital, I had a recurring dream. In the dream, there was a Japanese of enormous girth, stripped to the waist, barefoot, and carrying a knife. I knew that I had to find him before he found my family, or before he found me. I kept the sheath knife under my bed. I would stand in the dark, listening and hearing my heart beat, trying to breathe slowly. I moved very slowly from room to room. I stood and listened for a long time at each doorway. When my parents would finally light a lamp, I would wake up.

Gradually even these feelings were locked up again. The war began slipping away from memory. I was discharged from the army and placed on a small disability pension. For a month or so, I stayed in a small apartment in Ely, attending the local junior college on the GI bill. I thought that I should do some small thing to make the world a better place, but I had no idea of how to bring such a thing about.

During those first few months, the one thing that would bring out the war feelings would be to get together with friends who had actually been in combat. My uncle, now Marine Master Sergeant Claude Taylor, and I would invariably get around to talk of guns

137

and killing and acts of bravery and foolishness. For an hour or two, the pictures would come alive again, including memories of Guido, Charley, Bloody, and Sidello. Over the years, these interludes became less and less frequent. At some point as an adult, there were no longer any combat veterans around that could resurrect these feelings. Combat talk never focused on the depth of fear during a shelling, or the sense of shock from killing another human being, or the grief at losing a buddy. Even today, these feelings remained deeply locked away.

More than half a century later, I am still trying to get a perspective about the impact of combat on young warriors. The topic is also a matter of increasing professional attention. The last decade has brought a host of follow-up studies on combat veterans. These studies show that as young soldiers become mature adults, more than half of them show symptoms of Post Traumatic Stress Disorder. For some, this means feelings of anxiety, depression, and recurring combat-related dreams. The greater the amount of combat, the greater the risk for PTSD. It is obvious that being involved in combat does indeed carry with it an overload of poorly understood emotion. Obviously, locking away the post-combat memories is not good for young men. Perhaps what is needed is a psychologist in every foxhole coping with the emotions as they arise. Another solution, of course, would be to stop sending adolescents and each generation of young men (and now women) off to wars.

There is one further facet uncovered by contemporary studies: What keeps men in their foxholes and keeps them obeying orders to shoot or to charge the machine gun is not the flag. It is not the oath of allegiance. It is not the seeking of glory and honor. Rather, it is the mens' relationships with their buddies that drives them to remain in combat. Most men would climb a hill to where the enemy is waiting rather than let a buddy down. What this means is that war rests upon a perversion of one of the fundamental components of being human: love. In a very real sense, waging effective war has love as its base.

I still experience a sense of rage about my lost innocence; a sense that the best that was within me was used in an unworthy enterprise. I understand now that if I follow the orders of older, wiser men, I can be led yet again to another artillery barrage where all words about patriotism, love, and courage become meaningless. Today, all around the globe there are young men and women guarding muddy ridges and told to fire into a mass of humanity that somebody has identified as "the enemy."

Wrapped in Flags

In secret valleys, they gather,
 these men who are older,
and said to be wiser.
Divine seers of eminent threat,
they utter the magic words for War.
Young men asleep in summer grasses
are metamorphosed into Warriors.
They rush off to guard the passes
and the narrow ridges.

As a young man, I too guarded
 a narrow ridge of mud in a distant place.
The other Warriors found us there
 and came wrapped in flags
and a mist of words
 to make the last Banzai charge of that war.
We shot them as they came.
 The lines of bodies were covered
by a word mist and pieces of flags.
In their wallets were pictures,

but not enough to make a person.
At home, the older, wiser men
Were there proclaiming us to be heroes.
Wrapped in flags, we stood in a mist of words
and received our medals.

Now that I am sixty, they are charging again.
Again I shoot them dead,
and again,
                again.
But the flags are gone;
I can see now that they are men.
Their families stand and watch with sad, dark eyes
as I shoot.
Where is the word mist now?

I drag a cloak of dead faces.
Warriors from the narrow muddy ridges.
It keeps me from floating with clouds,
or flying with birds.

I know now that the killing game
was invented
by older men who are not wiser.
They gather now in deep valleys, all over the globe,
with their ready solution to problems

They only vaguely perceive.

(to Guido and Charlie)
Okinawa, 1945

6

Return to Quetico

When I returned to the lake area and enrolled in school, I found that the courses at the local junior college were not much different from high school. Both Bob Olson and I quickly became impatient with the slow pace of things there. His father was the dean of the junior college; but even so, he urged us to try something more challenging. He arranged for us both to be admitted in midterm to a small college in northern Wisconsin. Sig had once enrolled at Northland College when, as a young man, he had set out upon a similar quest.

I sat in my grandmother's house, waiting to be taken to a tiny city in northern Wisconsin. She gave me coffee as we waited and then said, "Here, Yeddy, you take dis for coffee along vay," and stuffed a ten-dollar bill into my shirt pocket. She stood at the screen door and waved, tears on her cheeks, "Ja, you be gute boy, Yeddy. Vork hard. Come home." I picked up the Duluth pack, the suitcase, and my cased shotgun, and boarded the Greyhound bus for Ashland, Wisconsin.

I was twenty years old. At the college, I would receive a Veteran's Administration check each month, which would cover my tuition and room and board. I felt a sense of excitement about going to a real college. During the long months in the army hospital, I had spent hours in their library. They could get any book that I wanted. I became excited by the idea of learning. I was interested in almost everything I read, but had no real sense of what was im-

141

portant and what was not. I did not know where to start. In the way of people from small towns, I struck up conversations and tried to form friendships with each of the persons randomly assigned to the seat next to mine.

That night the bus dropped me and several other young people off in front of Ashland's single hotel, about eight blocks away from Northland College. The streets were lined on both sides with huge elm trees and well-kept houses. I felt a mounting sense of excitement as I slowly walked up the hill. There were small groups of students coming down the sidewalk. I could see that I was dressed differently from them, in my basic uniform of Levi's, boots tied with the laces coming down in back, and a black leather jacket. I had also brought two pairs of army woolens, dyed green for dress up, a few shirts and sweaters, and three ties.

The campus sat on top of the hill, a tiny quadrangle defined by four buildings. Two of the buildings were quite old, and two were very new. I noticed that the campus had long ago been stripped of trees. I found the registrar's office, set the pack, the gun, and the suitcase in the hall, and began to fill out the necessary forms. No, it was not possible to sign up for advanced courses in the first year. It was required instead that I sign up for basic courses in English, trigonometry, and social studies.

Bob and I roomed together. We fed each other's excitement about learning, and both felt as if we had lost a great deal of time. I wanted to learn everything and I wanted to do it immediately. Both of us studied every spare moment during the day and for several hours each evening. For the first few months, we approached learning with a monkish dedication. The trajectory did not go unnoticed, that spring, both of us received Tojer Foundation awards for scholarship. For the first time in my life, I began to think of myself as someone dedicated to the world of ideas. I had found a new path, and with it, a new sense of self. The change was a surprise not only to me but to friends and family as well. In high school there had been a whole world of things competing with the world of ideas. At Northland, the world of ideas moved to center stage.

To add to that intensity, Bob and I were among the first of the returning veterans to appear on the campus. There were hundreds of young girls going through the molting process with but little assistance from their opposite kind. There were beautiful girl-women everywhere, and they constantly disrupted my efforts to concentrate upon the academic process. One night I had the great misfortune of cavorting in the snow with one of them during the very moment the Dean of Women walked across the campus bridge. She happened to glance up into the trees and saw myself and a lady friend heavily engaged. She suggested that perhaps I needed counseling. I thought that what I needed was a car. In due course, both Bob and I found suitable partners and became accepted parts of the campus scene.

Northland had a small campus. Eventually you met everybody. I soon discovered a small band of staff and students from the political science department that had similar interests to my own. They met informally in the coffee shops and in the homes of a few professors. To me, this small group represented the intellectual life of that place. They encouraged me to increase the load of courses I was taking and to sit in on classes that they were teaching. Professor Sharpe was at the center of this group. He taught history and political science. I could only dimly follow the seminars held in his home on Laski's theory of state, but I was excited by the ebb and flow of questions swirling about the tiny group in his living room. He did not seem to have a fixed position, but held himself and the group to consider alternative positions in depth. He was as excited as a young student when he found some new paper that related to the topics he was working on. He would come in flushed, eyes sparkling, and interrupt the ongoing discussion. "Excuse me," he'd start, "but let me read you this paragraph. I found it last night." Reading and pointing at the text with his finger, he would bend over the paper and then look up with a slight smile, turning his head as if listening to himself. "You see, it is just as we were saying last week." Each bit of knowledge felt new to him. It was alive. Ideas were like organic things that continued to grow.

He saw each of us as potential contributors to the ideas growing in his own mind. He was not a computer spewing facts to be memorized; he was somebody who was always in the process of learning. Each of us was permitted to help him grow, and in doing so, grew with him. I was honored by the experience; it was what I had always hoped college life would be like. As I later learned, Dr. Sharpe embodied the very essence of what a great college or university experience is all about. A small, gently rounded, middle-aged man, he had thick black hair that was neatly barbered, but still constantly fell forward over his glasses. He dressed in nondescript suits. If he was walking, he was in a hurry.

One day I saw him moving toward me through a crowd of students like a ship through water: head down and at top speed as usual. He stopped as he came abreast of me, flipping the hair from his glasses as he looked up. "Here. Please fill this out and bring it back to me in an hour. Can you do that?" I nodded, and he disappeared into the throng of students again. It was the midterm examination for one of his classes in medieval history. I was not taking the class, but I was immensely flattered that he would ask me to fill out the examination. Later, I learned that he was pleased that some untutored trapper from the north woods could take his examinations and score above average without taking the course. He used the score as a goad for his lecture classes, but had the good judgment to leave the perpetrator unidentified.

During my second semester, my relationship with Professor Sharpe subtly changed. The flow of the books he gave me to read steadily escalated. Many of the books were far in advance of my ability. Later, I was allowed to enroll in advanced courses for credit. I found myself taxed to the extreme. Every other week required an essay interpreting some complex historical event. On one such occasion, I chose to write an essay on the career of Joan of Lorraine. I had thought that I already knew more than a little about the events surrounding her. He handed out the papers with their grade, but withheld mine. I walked up after class to inquire about my essay. He handed it to me and said, "This would get a passing grade, but from you, such a performance is simply not acceptable. Please do it over again." He frowned, then turned and walked away from me. I was both flattered and crushed by the experience.

At Northland, I found time to ignite one of my several brief love affairs with music. A therapist at the Springfield Missouri Veterans hospital had told me that there was a chance that I could learn to move the other fingers on my left hand. He mentioned piano lessons as one approach. I signed up for piano lessons with Miss Ball. She was very sympathetic to what I was trying to do and nurtured me by finding novice renditions for some of the classic pieces that I loved. I found time each day to practice. By the end of the year, the left hand was more normal in appearance and looked less like some residual claw left over from another age. The piano was no longer a rehabilitation tool and I found myself looking forward to playing.

The small group of students I hung out with spent a good deal of time talking about the usual range of topics covered by undergraduates: the Koran, the Vedic hymns, the Bhagavad-Gita, as well as Hesse, Sartre, Camus, and the rest of the intellectual feast coming out of Europe at that time. I was an eager participant in coffeehouse discussions. Cass was one of my favorite contributors to these soirees. He seemed older than the rest of us, and with a well-developed sense of irreverence that the rest of us lacked. He characterized most of the coterie to which I belonged as "actors practicing to be geniuses."

Cass was very tall and thin with a black thatch of uncombed hair surmounting a huge grin. We met in the flooded swamps that were within walking distance of the campus. By wading waist-deep through the swamp, I had discovered that it concealed

145

mallard ducks. People tried to hunt them in boats, but they could not get close enough because the ducks could hear the boats coming. Wading was quiet enough so that it was possible to jump shoot a few ducks on the weekends. Cass had heard the shooting in the swamp and came down to investigate. It turns out that he was a duck hunter, too, and that he had also brought his gun to the campus. We eventually found that we enjoyed each other's company. Cass never indicated any interest in the group of "talker people" that I hung out with. He considered it to be a twisted and bent part of me that he had no wish to explore.

Horace walked over to the table where Cass and I sat. He was one of the advanced students and clearly a leading light among Cass's "talker people." Like Cass, he was a tall and thin, but he held himself very erect and dressed in the most elegant preppy style. He took the pipe from his mouth and eyed us disapprovingly. "I see the campus jocks are having a caucus," he asked. "Can I join?"

Cass laughed. "Only if you can meet the requirements for being a jock. Now first off, there . . ."

"Oh, Cass, stop that. Your ridiculous he-man crap bores the hell out of me."

Horace had left a large eastern university because, he claimed, they had been corrupted by their own success. He said he felt comfortable at Northland because of its frontier spirit and élan. He could often be found talking avidly in small groups of students. His breadth of knowledge was enormous, and somehow you always found yourself addressing one of his favorite topics. This was his second year trying to write his senior's honors thesis, a fact which had led Professor Sharpe to make several caustic comments.

After a brief interval Horace left. I turned to watch him go, "Christ, he is smart. He is some kind of genius. He knows something about everything. I have never brought up a topic he didn't know more about than I did."

Cass laughed, "Yeah, you are looking at his life's work. He spends all of his time working on that to get you to say he is a genius. But he is all words and no go. He will go nowhere. He is one of my branded-by-genius guys."

I looked at him in surprise. "What does that mean, branded by genius?"

Cass was grinning and waving at people as they walked by. "They are like a beautiful calliope that makes great music, but never goes anywhere. Every one of them has been told that they are a genius. They have been told that all their life. Ultimately, that is what screws them up. When they have to lay it on the line, they know right away that they can't produce the earth-shattering piece of work that everyone expects." Later I was to meet a great many advanced cases of Cass's "branded-by-genius."

I returned to Robinson Lake that spring, stuffed with the progress I thought I had made. I was shocked to discover that no one in the family was interested in what I had learned. They approved of my going to school, but had no need to hear about the details. The real questions they were interested in were things like: Are you still a good person? Do you care about us? Still love the bush? My uncles and cousins were much more interested in the question of whether I was still in good physical condition. Each hug or handshake was an exploratory maneuver to determine my level of physical fitness. The more degrees I earned, the larger the number of cousins assigned to throwing me off the dock and into the lake as part of the homecoming ceremony.

When I came home from college that first spring in my new life, I had an important question to answer. I went to the cabin at Robinson Lake knowing my mother and father were not at home, took the 18-foot Old Town Guide's Model canoe out of the garage. I laid it on a patch of bare ground and walked around it. I was a beautiful old V-Z hull. There were the two ribs we had patched with pieces of heavy-gauged tin. There were the canvas patches I had put on after the last trip. The question was, could I pick it up?

147

Would two fingers be enough to hold the top gunwale as I use my right arm to flip it up on my shoulder? I didn't know. The doctors hadn't the vaguest notion of what I was asking them when I had brought the question up: "*What do you mean, you throw the canoe over your head?*" I looked around to be sure that I was alone and bent down to begin the ritual. First, move the canoe on its side and lean against it with both knees. Then grasp the center thwart with both hands and slide it, balanced evenly, up on my lap. I sat leaning back and cradling my friend for a second, then slipped my right hand and arm deep around its bottom. The canoe was balanced and still. Then I reached up with my left hand and grasped the gunwale with the two fingers. The rest of the sequence ran itself off automatically. The hull lifted to shoulder height. As it did, I twisted my feet and torso beneath it so that the yolk skipped over my head and landed precisely on my shoulders. I shouted with relief and then moved down to the dock and to the patch of black water showing a small area in the ice. The sequence was reversed, and I slid the canoe into the water and then tied it off.

I went to get the paddles. There was one more crucial question to be answered: Could two fingers and a crooked wrist control the paddle enough to do the job? I stepped into the canoe and kneeled in front of the rear thwart. The canoe drifted out into the black water. I tried to paddle first on the right side. But given the fixed position of my left wrist, I could not get a precise control in feathering the blade either in or out of the water. Both movements require a subtle wrist motion with the left hand that was now impossible. That meant that in rapids or a high wind, I could not work from the right side.

I shifted the paddle to the left side of the canoe. The thumb and forefinger circled the paddle low on its haft. The wrist bent back in its position could be corrected by simply shortening the stroke. This could be done by simply not reaching forward with the blade, but starting with the shaft almost vertical. I stroked and the canoe surged forward and began, as expected, to arc toward the right. The J-stroke corrected for this and, as expected, the canoe shot across the small opening in a straight line. Finally, there was only one other question. I knelt in the center of the canoe and tried the 360 pivot maneuver. The stroke uses only one face of the paddle. By rotating the shaft of the paddle in a circle, the canoe should slowly turn in a full 360 degree circle without moving from its position in the wind. The wrist and finger hurt with the effort, but the canoe slowly spun in its circle. In the bright blue sky, two crows answered the loud shouts from the tiny figure sitting in his canoe in the first water of spring.

In mid-June four of us decided to make a spring training run to the eastern edge of the map. My thirteen-year-old brother Mike was in the bow of my canoe. A Robinson Lake neighbor, Lyman Childers, paddled in the other canoe. The stern man had volunteered to come along just to see the country. Bill Rom, our other volunteer, was planning to open what later became one of the most successful outfitting operations in Ely's history.

Our two canoes traveled from sunup to sundown every day. We were a company of young men testing ourselves and each other. By the end of the second day, we were in the northern reaches of Agnes. By the third, we had passed through the dour, burnt-over Kawnipi land, and pushed our way up into the swamps and muskeg of the Wawiag River. Our destination was Mack Lake, to the east. The trip was an orgiastic outpouring of energy. There was much laughing. Each day we paddled too far and ate too much. I was home! This was still my primary path. It was still here, I still belonged and still felt like part of it all. I knew now that my left arm would be no problem. The trip had tightened up muscles grown lax from the months spent in the hospital.

It was a clear, warm day. Wearing almost-new boots and my almost-new Levi's, I walked into the Canoe Country Outfitters to see if they had any trips scheduled for me. As soon as I came in the door, Bernie began. "Hey, John, HE'S here." John, whom I had not seen for two years, rushed from the back of the warehouse and

149

ignored my outstretched hand as he circled me in a hug. "You are one lucky son of a bitch, but even Lucky Pierre can have too much of a good thing." John and Bernie were both grinning and laughing and raising such a hullabaloo that several tourists trying to buy some fishing tackle became alarmed and edged toward the door. Finally Bernie let up and shook my hand, "Welcome back, Jer." Bernie's casual greeting was the first sensible thing that had happened since I walked through the door. "Incidentally, what is it that I'm supposed to do, and what are those lobotomy cases giggling about?" Bernie walked over to the counter, flipped open a file folder, and took out a letter. "There is this woman, Jackie, who is bringing twenty-one adolescent girls up for a five-day trip. They asked specifically for you. You, Lucky Pierre, are it." Bernie handed me the letter and gave me the biggest shit-eating grin you ever saw.

Ely is a small town, party-line telephones made it even smaller. As I spent the next two days selecting four 18-foot and six 16-foot canoes and packing the gear, there was a constantly shifting group of advisors in attendance. The advice and the offers given varied: Tommy Aho and his brother offered to paddle behind us just out of sight and then take turns at night in my tent so that I could get some rest. Others suggested that I circle endlessly in North Bay and never portage out of it just to conserve my strength. For two days, I was an unwilling participant in a singular fantasy shared by Ely's randy males of all ages. People I didn't even know grinned at me on the street.

The morning the girls were to arrive by chartered bus, it seemed like there were an unconscionably large number of Ely men with nothing to do but circulate in the canoe warehouse. They drifted in and out the front door and clustered on the sidewalk in front. There were little clots of horny men all up and down the street. John burst through the door, "Bill, Bill, they're here. Big bus coming down Sheridan Street right now." The bus stopped front of the Outfitters. The bus windows were filled with faces of girls with brown hair, red hair, blonde hair—every kind of girl that you could imagine. All eyes were on the girls at the windows. A figure in a chauffeur's hat–who bore a disturbing resemblance to the staff sergeant at Fort Hood—he even had a drill sergeant type voice which rose above the babble of twenty-one girls descending from the bus, as he shouted, "Who runs this place?" Then the chauffeur's hat came off and revealed that the source of the voice was actually a woman. The figure flipped a huge duffel bag over her shoulder and marched smartly inside. There was a moment of silence from the surrounding crowd. A dozen rich fantasies died aborning.

I was the guide, but there was no doubt that Jackie the ladies' head honcho was in command. No, she did not want to take an easy trip. These girls were members of an elite Explorers group. By definition, they were inured to hardship of all kinds. Yes, of course they could carry canoes and packs; all of them were experienced at portaging. No, they would not sleep in three or four large tents; they had brought their own two-person pup tents; in fact they had brought twelve of them. It would be up to me to find campsites large enough to accommodate that many tents.

As we loaded the packs into the truck in back of the warehouse, Bernie reminded me of the fate of one of Ely's most historic figures. Apparently in all the fifty years of canoe guides there had been only one who had strayed. When that guide considered the choice between his mummy bag and a mummy bag that included one of the women from his party, he chose the latter. His name has long since been forgotten, for afterwards he was assigned to work in the deepest shaft of the iron mine and had to support this family in the summertime by trapping squirrels.

We left early in the morning for the landing at Moose Lake. Two trucks pulled the canoe trailers. All of the girls were secured in the bus with Jackie. At the lake, Jackie assigned individuals to canoes. My 18-foot canoe lay heavy in the water; a sturdily constructed red-headed girl sat in the center and a stunning nymphet manned the bow. The objective for the day was to get to the large island on the south side of Bailey Bay, where there would be room enough to contain our small village of tents. However, for me, the journey itself took place in a miasma of hormones constantly stimulated by a half-revealed breast here, a bare thigh there, and the overweening distractions of T-shirts, halters, and tight Levi's. The conversation during that day and the ones that followed did not have the same solid concreteness of, "How deep is it here?", "Are there bear there?", or "What do you do in the wintertime in this country?"

There was no one at the island when we arrived. I took charge of stacking the food packs and setting up the kitchen in the usual way. Jackie took charge of protecting her brood. The girls pitched their tents around the open clearing next to the kitchen area. As I started to put up my own tent in the same area, Jackie suggested that it might be better if I put it down at the other end of the island; it would give them more privacy. I pointed out that I usually slept by the food packs because of the bears. She snorted and strode over to her pack. "We don't have to worry about bears," she said, and with a deft movement she reached down and pulled out a 45 Colt automatic, pulled the action back to a cock position, and held it at the ready.

Each night after dinner, the little group led by Jackie would file down to my end of the island. Then we would have the required number of stories and campfire songs. At the end of the pre-arranged time, she would lead them back to the protection of her end of the world. Each night I prayed the bears would come and work their way with Jackie. Maybe at the sight of a huge black snout poking through her tent door and she would crack at the edges and scream. If she didn't leave, I would at least be a hero when I chased the bear away. No bears came. No other fantasies were realized either. Not one.

We arrived at North Bay, the end of the lake, and also the beginning of three or four canoe routes. On entering our route, we had to execute our first tiny portage, which had the same effect as stirring up a column of ants. There were figures hurrying in every direction with not the least semblance of order. What Jackie had meant by girls carrying canoes was four of them carrying a single boat at one time. My God, what if my friends saw me on a portage with a party doing that! The first platoon of four girls and one boat started up the hill before I was able to land my canoe. They slipped and got stuck in mid-portage because the trail was not cut wide enough for two people to walk side by side, let alone two people trying to drag a canoe between them. So stuck, the first group blocked the portage trail. A dozen figures were scurrying through the brush to get around them, carrying paddle and tackle boxes in each hand. Several carried just armfuls of blouses, hats, and dangling shoes.

At this point, a beautifully organized column of Scouts returning from an extended trip came over the top of the hill. Jackie and I were everywhere; each with a different purpose. I began by stacking piles of gear at each end. I shouted instructions as I carried each of the remaining canoes over the portage. Jackie was everywhere, sheep-dogging the alder brush on each side of the trail. She was frantic. She could see brush on both sides of the trail reflecting the movements of Scouts and girls. Hopefully, none of these reflected coordinated movements. It was a housemother's worse nightmare. The Scouts were thoroughly aware of the drama in the situation. Some were standing in the water to help damsels load and unload their packs, while others, perhaps the less observant, offered to help me carry the nine canoes. I barked savagely at them and pushed Sisyphus-like up the hill.

The scout leader came over to me as they were pulling off into North Bay. "Aren't you Jerry Patterson, the guide that worked at the Scout base a while back?" he asked, standing there in moccasins with no socks on, long knife at his belt and even longer sash, trying not to laugh. "Yeah, I'm him," I said and walked back up the hill, knowing that my reputation as Courrier de Bois had been lost forever in this welter of disorganized femininity.

For a year or two, I wrote back and forth with several of the young women who had been on the trip. But one by one, they discovered other young men, who were equally eager and much more available. Fifteen years later, I was giving a lecture at the University of Minnesota and noticed a woman patiently waiting until the last obdurate questioner had left. She stood up and walked over to me. "Are you Jerry Patterson, from the Quetico?" she asked. We talked then about how marvelous it was to have shared an infatuation in that setting and at that time in our lives. I did not mention that I was still searching for a partner in my travels. My image was of a woman, not a nymphet, sitting in the bow of a canoe and moving away with me to some far-off place. Someone who would come to the edge of the map and still want to keep going.

The fishermen began arriving in June, just a few weeks after my experience with the girls. I spent weeks in the big lake trout water at McIntyre and Brent, the old places. Some of my private campsites, hidden in back bays, had not been used since I left. In one, I even found the beaver wood I had stacked when I left to go to war. Piece by piece, I began assembling a new life. Okinawa and the war slipped far away.

A summer's worth of work guiding had finally become lucrative, and the family at Robinson Lake seemed to decide that canoe guiding may have been a reasonable choice, after all. Each season meant a hundred days in the bush at top wages, plus free "room and board." Each fall I would bring what for me was a small fortune to college. During the summers, I could take my pick of parties from each of the three major outfitters: Border Lakes, Bill Rom's Canoe Country Outfitters, and Wilderness Outfitters. Many of my old parties were returning year after year. Each summer became a congress of old friends and reunions. I also began to work with various guides taking out larger groups. I began working with a new generation of canoe guides, such as Joe Santineau.

Joe was my friend Jim's younger brother, but the newer version was so huge that he looked more like a barge man than a canoe man. We were sitting in the guide's shack at Wilderness Lodge on Basswood when I mentioned this to him. I thought I was being humorous. The four of us had been lake guiding and, at the end of the day we had asked the pilot of the pontoon plane to bring us a bottle of whiskey when he came back from Ely. This was to be our last day there. We were passing the bottle and dipping into the water pail for chasers. The bottle had passed around several times before my remark slipped out. When I said it, Joe got up abruptly and took off his thick glasses. He stood well over six feet and looked a good way past two hundred thirty pounds. His shift produced a moment of dead silence. As he started in my direction one of the other guides said, "Christ, you blind moose, you are going to break something."

Joe shuffled around the circle with a tiny smile on his face, "I'm just going to break this candy-ass canoe guide; just put his ass outside with the bears where he belongs." The circle cleared immediately, and the bottle of booze disappeared into the little ring of spectators.

As I rose up to meet him, I put my foot in a pail; definitely not a good beginning. I kicked it out of the way, and we grabbed each other around the waist. I couldn't move him. I could feel that he was about to put a permanent bow in my ribs. I put all my weight against his right shoulder. We were both puffing, not quite sure whether this was a game or not. As he pushed back against me, I stepped away quickly, and he stumbled forward, spinning as he went. I moved around him, trying to get a headlock on him, but he was just too tall and too strong. I kept moving him backward and around in a little dance that knocked the table over, then removed the pot-bellied wood stove from its mountings. Neither of us was getting anywhere with the other. Joe finally broke my hold around his waist and we stood facing each other, panting, about five feet apart. Then he simply lowered his head and shoulders and took me waist high, a great block. We both sailed through the screen door, taking it neatly off its hinges. The cheering section around us crowded into the lighted doorway, surveyed us, and pushed the bottle to us. "You guys ain't getting your share, sitting on your asses out there in the dark." We both rose, and went back inside to finish the party.

After that, Joe and I worked together on several canoe trips. I liked his big, easygoing ways. Laughing came easily to him, and he seemed to have none of the dark thoughts that for some guides accumulate over a trip. I had already established that he tended to be a bit confrontational when he was drinking. At one point we were hired by Fred Handburg, the owner of a spanking new outfitting company on Moose Lake, to take out a party of three lake trout fishermen. Fred asked us to take them into the Knife Lake and Kekakabic country to try for big lake trout.

Fred Handburg was a short, wide, intense person. He let us know that he was very serious about giving first-class service to this high-priced group from Chicago. This was his first year in business and his buildings were set right on the shores of Moose Lake. That made it very convenient for starting and ending one's trips. I particularly liked to take parties out from there because my brother Mike drove the launch to Prairie Portage, and the trip gave us several hours to visit. Mike was taller than I, but built lean like Dad. He kept his hair cut short so that no one could see his tight blond curls. We spent hours planning our someday canoe trip to Hudson's Bay.

At Handburg's, everything was new: the tents, the canoes, and even the packs had the store smell clinging to them. Fred brought in the party from Ely in the truck. He hovered in the background as Joe Santineau and I talked with them about what they wanted to do. He kept dancing in and out of the group, checking to be sure that Joe's and my laughing and joking didn't mean that we weren't serious about the trip. He mentioned several times what great fishermen our fathers were.

With one thing and another, we got a very late start, and it was well into the afternoon before we paddled the two canoes down Moose Lake, heading for the campsite between Birch and Carp Lake. This was not the greatest place in the world to camp because it was only a few yards from the portage trail, but there really wasn't much choice. We pitched the camp right along the river, about halfway across the portage. It was a nice camp, a clear warm day, and everyone was feeling the excitement of the first day of the trip. Joe and I had worked out a system of one man pitching the tents while the other set up the kitchen and got the pots boiling.

Joe came back to the kitchen where I was working. One of the party gave him a healthy belt of booze in a tin cup. He sat watching me for a while, then looked over at the rapids. "Betcha five bucks you can't run that mother." I looked up, and there was that nasty flinty smile on his face, and the thick glasses, little black slits for eyes. I looked over at the rapids. It really wasn't much of a river; it was more like a short bobsled run of a hundred feet or so that eventually dropped through a rock garden. There was a huge granite boulder at the very bottom of the chute. It was the bottom that was the problem. There was just barely room for a canoe to slip by the boulder that sat in the middle of the river. It would have to be precisely done, but it should have been easy. No one had ever talked about running it.

"Tell you what, I'll bet you ten dollars you can't bash and mash your way through that." This was casual banter; both of us knew that we were not going to do that river. You simply don't run rapids when you are guiding a party. One of the party didn't know that, and suddenly changed the bet for both of us. He said, "I'll bet you both twenty that you can't make it." We were both silent. There was no way around that challenge. If we sidestepped it, we had lost face for the remainder of the trip. We sighed and rose to our feet.

"I'll get the canoe, Joe; get three paddles. I'll meet you at the top of the chute."

Joe was heaviest, so he knelt in the back and I knelt in the front. "Okay, let's do it," I said. The current whipped us into midstream, and before we had enough momentum for steering we ground to a momentary halt on a rock that lay just under the water. Then we were under way again. Whitewater canoeing techniques did not exist then, so our strategy only was to paddle furiously to get more speed than the current. If you can do this, then theoretically you can turn in fast water. The canoe did not feel like it was under control. It was yawing this way and that. Each time I tried to steer around the big rock at the bottom, the canoe remained pointed firmly in that direction. I glanced back and saw Joe on his hands and knees. He yelled, "Goddamn glasses." His glasses had slid off at the first impact. I turned back to see that we were rushing right into the boulder guarding the lower stream. We hit it—a glancing blow on the left side. The force tossed me neatly out of the canoe and into the deep water below.

As I swam back I could see the river having its way with the new aluminum canoe. It was gently folding the canoe into a permanent embrace around the rock. I looked for Joe but did not see him. The members of the party were laughing and cheering. I saw his arm come out of the water. He was still in the canoe! I raced to the stern and tried lifting it off, but I could not move it. I screamed at the party, "He's drowning, help me!" They reacted as if to a joke, and there was more laughing, but nobody moved toward the river. I pulled myself over to Joe's end of the canoe. I touched his arm and said, "Joe, Joe, I'll get it off." I braced my feet against the rock and pulled myself literally under water. I could see him. The water formed a fuzzy window between us. He had his legs under the thwart, and the water had flattened it against the bottom of the canoe and the rock. I could not move the canoe. I reached for his arm when suddenly he shot from the water like some great whale—rising several feet, red and purple in the face. We helped each other trudge slowly to shore.

"I thought you were a goner for sure, Joe. How in hell did you get out of there?"

Puffing as he walked, he said, "I bent the fucking thwart with my legs."

We ran a rope down to one end of the canoe and pried and shimmied it off the rock. We hauled it up on shore, and then had the group jump on it to straighten it out. After finishing supper, Joe and I took the remaining canoe and tied the flattened husk across the middle. It hung out on either side. We opened a reserve bottle of bourbon and slowly paddled our way into the night. We reran the rapids run many times, sang songs, and drank the bourbon as we retraced the day's route back to the dock at Moose Lake. By the time we arrived at the outfitting company, we were in great spirits. We hauled the canoe remnant up on the dock and laid it like some sort of sacrificial offering beneath Fred's window. Then we stood, arms around each other's shoulders, gently rocking. "Fred. Fred. Hey, Fred, we are back! Oh, Fred. Hey, Fred, where are you, Fred?" The lights suddenly blazed all around us and the window slammed open. I never knew that he slept with a nightcap, but there it was. He glared down at us scowling, "What in hell are you guys . . . Where is the partyyyYYYY . . ." His voice broke and rose to a shriek as he saw the canoe.

The new canoe that we towed back down the lake came out of our wages for the trip. The remainder of the trip was subdued. The fishing wasn't great, either. Two decades later, a scholar that I knew was taking his family on a canoe trip in the boundary waters. They were all packed up and ready to start their trip when the manager of the outfitting company, Bernie Carlson, said, "Wait a minute; there is something I want you to see." He took them to a warehouse behind the main building, turned on the lights, and pointed to the crumpled shape mounted on a wooden pedestal. "You see that. That was a brand new canoe that one of our guides used to run a rapids. As you can see, neither he nor the canoe was up to the job." My colleague asked him how it had happened.

159

Bernie not only gave him the details, but also the names of the perpetrators. It's reassuring to think that our wages for that trip have gone into the construction of a small battered monument that keeps thousands of tourists from following in our footsteps.

Bernie Carlson and I also used to guide together, and had in fact, enjoyed more than our fair share of fast water ourselves. But I can see that for Bernie, maturity carries with it a new perspective. Each time I would come by the Outfitters, the story was retold.

During the summer, I made a particular point to visit Sig and his wife Elizabeth's elegant home up on the ridge to the south of Ely. The warm welcome backed up with coffee and cinnamon rolls was always reassuring. In their company, I was encouraged to talk about what I was learning and where it was that I was going. I would also get the latest news about Bob and his wife, Vonnie. Stories in the local newspapers made it evident that Sig was becoming internationally famous, both as a writer and an environmentalist. After coffee, we would go out to his writing shack behind the house. That is where he kept his maps for the trips to the wilderness country in northern Manitoba and Saskatchewan. Their trips required weeks of travel; most of them involved a good deal of technical whitewater to be run. He spoke of the Churchill and the Hayes Rivers, and country even further north in the N.W. Territories.

The fall storms were approaching; it was time for Dr. Bob Stewart to arrive. John and I had set out for the Moose Lake landing late in the afternoon. Together we set the packs along the gravel beach. Then we unstrapped the canoe and lifted it down from the top of the truck. John was a tall, thin man, his entire silhouette seemingly dominated by the enormous Adam's apple and a beaked nose. He had given up guiding when he married, there just wasn't enough steady money in it. He loved the bush, though, and it was good being with him when he spoke of the places that he had been. He looked up at the pack of cumulus clouds racing above us and the birch trees bending and stirring the wind. "Great day for it," he said. "Wish I was going with you. If you get to Fauquier, stay at my old campsite." He turned the truck and ground his way up the steep ridge in low gear.

Dr. Bob had arrived an hour earlier with another party that had already pulled out. He walked over to me with a huge grin, waved his arms, and shouted, hello. Bright pools of light moved over a darkening landscape, the clouds opening and closing like the lens on a camera. Where the sun hit along the shoreline, the whole landscape sprung to life in brilliant yellows and reds. My wool shirt felt good, and the food packs had that full blend of rich smells coming from them that they always give off on the first day of a trip. "Waves are not too big today, Courrier de Bois?" he asked. He gave me a big grin as he moved about, putting the paddles in their places.

"Ah, my bookish friend from the city; today I have a surprise for you. Do you notice that the canoe is loaded differently?" The heavy food packs were loaded forward. The canoe was riding heavy in the bow. I placed yet another pack in front of the bow seat.

Bob looked quizzical. "Leaving me here on the beach is a bit of surprise."

"No, in this operation you are really needed. Hold the canoe for a second, and I will construct the surprise." With that, I cut an 8 foot mast from the alder brush along the shore, and then a smaller diameter crosspiece. Both pieces were cut to fit the measurements of an army surplus rain poncho: this was the Quetico version of a running sail fit for a canoe.

I paddled the canoe out and around the first small point. Dr. Bob sat in the middle holding the mast with its sail flapping about in the water. "I like the surprise. A nice change of pace from the toil and grind you have arranged in the past." We were in position now, the wind coming up from behind us and driving small black waves before it. There was an occasional white breaker far out in the middle.

161

"Lift the sail. This is the wind that launched a thousand canoes." After much silent pulling and puffing, Dr. Bob had the mast pulled up and braced in the curve of the yoke. His heels were braced in against the butt of the mast at its bottom. The wind caught the sail with a swoop. The right side had already been tied off with a slip knot. I adjusted the left side to fit the direction of the wind. At first the sounds from the movement came only as whispers. Then with a joyful sound, the canoe picked up speed. Small waves began slapping against the bow and gradually built to the hissing melody of fast-moving water.

Dr. Bob looked ecstatic. "What a great beginning!" We swooped like a gull through the narrow passage into Newfound Lake. As we came into Prairie Portage, we scattered a small covey of tourists in their rented motor boats. They pulled aside to make way for a sailing vessel, as was only proper.

It was good to be crossing that threshold again, particularly with Dr. Bob, who could fully participate in the experience. We rode the wind north through most of the day. In spite of the black-bottomed clouds, very little rain fell. By mid-afternoon, we were well into the big water, and the wind began to get real purchase on the waves. We would be pulled up one wave and then yaw badly as we rode down the other side. We rode on the edge of things for another mile and then both decided to give the wind a rest and take down the sail. We paddled into one of the deep bays and found a small island sheltered from the wind. That evening we opened a bottle and began the conversation that would last the week.

I asked him, for the first time, what his life was like outside of this place. He told me that he ministered to a large church in Wheaton, Illinois. I was shocked, because there was little about him that I usually associated with a man of the cloth. I had assumed that he was a professor of some kind, maybe a psychiatrist or a philosopher. I began to sense that important things were miss-

162

ing from his life, but I was too inexperienced to get a sense of what they might be.

He was deeply interested in my experiences in Okinawa and gently questioned me about it several times. I had no real story to tell. There were only disconnected experiences. The images were overlaid with a blur of feelings that I could not label. "The thing I don't understand, Dr. Bob; I killed people, a lot of people. What happened to the feelings? I lost a lot of friends; where is the grief? I don't really know what happened out there. Why is it so disconnected?"

Dr. Bob was leaning forward toward the fire, holding the cup of brandy over his knee, and speaking very softly more to himself than to me. "Yes, that is strange. War carries with it a lot of unfinished business. But imagine if every time a buddy was killed, the entire squad went into grieving as a family might do. Each casualty would require several days of grieving. Such an army would not work. The militarists must have discovered that long ago."

We both fell silent, and then he continued, telling me about new studies coming out of the National Institutes of Health. The studies pointed to the idea of unfinished business, and found that 60 percent of combat veterans are diagnosed with symptoms of post traumatic stress disorders by the time they reach age fifty! As if it all goes underground for a quarter of a century. There was a part of me that went along with the newspaper account of each combat veteran being a hero. There was another part that felt violated, as if I had been raped. It was something that I could not put into words because it made no sense at all.

The next morning the mist lay thick in the bay. The island and the countryside were embraced by this quiet lover, and the surface of the lake was absolutely calm. The loons moved in pairs through the fog, making strange little worried cries to each other as they circled, looking for familiar landmarks. I had awakened early, and sat on a log by the fire having my first cup of coffee. As I walked over to Dr. Bob's tent, the fog hanging a hundred feet above our

163

heads was suddenly illuminated. As the sun came over the ridge far to the east, the fog-sky became translucent, gently pulsating to the air currents moving about. "Good morning, Dr. Bob," I said into the tent. "Coffee! Take a quick look outside. It's a gorgeous morning." A thin, bony hand and wrist appeared to take the coffee cup by the door, but from within, there was only silence.

As I started breakfast, the deeply wrinkled boy's face appeared. "You are right, a great morning. What should we do today?"

"We could make it into the deep bush today, but only if you really feel like traveling. What is your pleasure?" By the time breakfast was over, the sun had taken all of the mist, but the air was very still. Voices could be heard from far across the big water to the west of us.

We followed the familiar lake systems from Sunday, then over the mile portage to Meadow. On the portage, I passed two of Joe Chosa's favorite resting spots: the first came right after the climb over the high ridge, and the second just before we started down into the last, short swamp. I could visualize him gliding along with the canoe and pack in his fast shuffling dance. Joe spent all of his time lake guiding now. He didn't come back into the bush much anymore.

Dr. Bob and I had lunch at the bathtub in the middle of Louisa Falls. I had taken Mr. Strauss here on my first guided trip; the portage went straight up the steep ridge on the right side of the falls. Dr. Bob carried one pack at a time up the trail and set them beside the canoe. I made lunch for us by the tub. We had sat in the tiny pool, holding onto the rocks in front of us. The water dropped twenty feet down the cliff to fall on our shoulders and backs. It was so cold that it took your breath away, and all that you could do was shout in protest. We took the teapot over to the one bright patch of sunlight allowed through the huge trees. Dr. Bob sat on a rock with his wool shirt over his bare shoulders, shivering and laughing. He grinned. "Actually, this would do a lot of my friends some good.

First a ten-mile paddle, a mile portage, and then climb this god-awful cliff with a pack a half-dozen times. Finally, sit and let yourself be pounded by a waterfall. All guaranteed to scrape away the scales and the coating left by the diseases of the city."

The Fauquier country is centered in the lower quadrant of the Quetico. It sits off by itself, a dark, brooding country surrounded by a tangle of swamps. It is high country; you are climbing all the way to get there. You pass through the high cliffs and Norway pine around Agnes, then climb to Lake Louisa. As you push beyond Louisa, the country changes imperceptibly to something quite different. The portage trails are seldom used, so they are difficult to find. They are overgrown, with a collection of fallen timbers that you go over, under, or around. There was one section where nothing worked except to get on your knees and crawl under a fallen tree with the canoe balanced on your shoulders. The trails seem to end in awkward places at the edges of swamp and by downed trees. The feeling there is bush—real high-country bush. It was a place of dark mystery, few campsites, and very deep water.

This was the last trip of the season, and I wanted to go there and say goodbye to things. I also wanted to introduce Dr. Bob to a part of the Quetico that he had not yet seen. I had brought my father's short trout rod with me. It had a star drag reel with two hundred yards of Monel line ideal for lake trout. We had spent the entire day moving from Lake Louisa up into the high country. Finally, we were floating in the secluded bay at the south end of the lake. All that you could see were small rock shelves, scrubby jack pine, and sections of swampy shoreline. I was putting the trout rod together as we floated out into the bay. "I can understand why there are not a lot of people here," Dr. Bob said.

He turned to see what I was doing. "What is this? Are you going to fish?"

"No. Dr. Bob, as a personal favor, I ask you to fish. We need to catch just one good-sized lake trout for the two-day rest stop in this place. It is for some very special cooking I must do for both of us." He did not give in easily. First I had to convince him that, for this fishing, everything lay in the skill of the paddler, not the fisherman. He finally acquiesced.

We did not even stop to unload the canoe at John's camp. Instead, we swung out into the open water on the west side of the lake. We made huge circles over the reef that ran from the point on its north end on a north-south axis down in 60 to 70 feet of water. Dr. Bob was clearly unhappy with the intense focus he had to give the bottom of the lake.

"Do you feel the sinker? It should start to bounce along the bottom about now."

He sat bent over the short rod, mumbling to himself. "Lord, there is no privacy at all for the fisherman. The guide burrows into your thoughts and demands that you concentrate on a blob of lead at the bottom of the lake." I kept him at it for an hour or two, relentlessly circling in the lake. The sun was almost touching the horizon when he said, "I'm stuck on the bottom again, sorry." I turned the canoe and started back to where I thought the hook was snagged. I had moved a good way back across the lake with Dr. Bob reeling in line, but the angle of the line stayed pretty much the same.

"Bob, in your innocence, you may have snagged a fish." I stopped paddling and he continued to reel in the line. At that point, the pole began pulsing, and he had to hold onto the rod with both hands as the fish took line from the reel. "Dr. Bob, just keep reeling even though he is taking line. That is a special reel. He can take line at the same time that you are bringing it in." The giving and taking went on for some time. Dr. Bob was tiring. He had been reeling in line continuously for a long time. Finally, I could see the flash of silver deep in the water immediately below us. "Dr. Bob, get ready. He will run soon now, and he will pull hard." The fish sighted the canoe and immediately responded with a long run amid a mixed chorus of groans and cheers, depending upon which end of the canoe was reacting. This time the fish came to the surface, but unlike most lake trout in those circumstances, he did not just float on his side gasping for air. Instead, he came out of the water, all fifteen pounds of him. Dr. Bob grabbed his reel with both hands and in doing so accidentally tightened the drag so that the fish could not take any more line. The fish put on an Olympic jumping performance all around the canoe. Much of the time he was as high out of the water as I was.

"Lake trout never do that."

Dr. Bob was clutching his reel, "I don't care what they never do. You do something." I shouted as I pivoted the canoe away from the trout, "Give line, loosen the star drag," I ordered. Finally, the fish was taking line again. When he tired, we both sat looking at the enormous fish floating belly-up by the canoe. The sun had gone down and the black shadows reached out to us from the shore.

I paddled us slowly over to the campsite. Dr. Bob sat staring at the lake. "It is a lovely thing, that fish. I'm deeply sorry that we had to kill it."

I continued to paddle. "Me too. Right now, lake trout for dinner doesn't seem like such a great idea." We made camp in silence. Dr. Bob pitched both of the tents in the darkness and then came to sit back against a rock by the fire. He mixed each of us a drink and then watched as I parboiled two huge chunks of lake trout and set the baking powder biscuits in the reflector oven. "Want something to nibble on, Dr. Bob? This meal is going to take awhile."

He sipped the mix of rum, butter, and hot water. "No, I'll wait. It will taste better that way."

"Drink your medication and wait for the fish cakes a la Faquier."

He looked over my shoulder and nodded with his cup. "I see you arranged the evening's entertainment. A gorgeous full moon." A huge golden searchlight cut a path across the black surface of the lake. The moon rose like a huge bubble above the black tips of the East Ridge.

"Always makes me restless, that kind of moon. If we were on big water, I'd want to pack the camp and travel tonight."

I mixed some dehydrated potatoes that he had brought from Chicago with diced onions, flour, and flakes of meat from the lake trout. The fish cakes were cooking on the aluminum griddle as I set the table and put the butter out for the biscuits. The canned corn set in a pot of boiling water. The molten light had reached across the lake now, and shafts of light were piercing the tree cover at camp. The loons in first one lake and then another mounted a ragged chorus. Both of us were sitting on the ground, knees folded like supplicants before our plates.

"See, it makes them restless too. Mrs. Loon is saying, 'Why don't you ever take me out? Let's fly over to Lake Agnes and see the Smiths. Why don't we ask my mother to come and visit?' "

Dr. Bob smiled, and tasted the fish cakes. "Great food. Thank you, lake trout." Each of us concentrated then on the food, sipping the rum drink, and watched the moonlight stroking the water. Nothing more was needed.

Behind me, Dr. Bob bent to the dishwashing ritual. He was grumbling and talking softly to himself. "God knows that guides are a talented lot, but why is it that it takes so many dirty pots to make a good meal? They travel to glory on a succession of black and greasy pots. I love fish cakes, but I'm sure an Indian could do it all with one pot." I took my drink and moved down to the rock slab jutting out over the water. Later, Dr. Bob came down and looked out over the lake. "Will you return to Northland College in the fall?"

"Yes, I think so. I may not stay, but I will go back."

He nodded, "Yes, crucial decisions, going and staying. It's all about change. It's all about process. If you go to school in the fall, you put yourself on an escalator that changes you over time. We are being changed all the time as we move along a dozen escalators that we have chosen. The problem is that we have no language, no way of thinking about the process." Both of us

168

understood that I had already begun moving away from Robinson Lake, yet neither of us had a sense of what the new path might be.

Dr. Bob was right. At first, change came in bits and pieces. Later, it was like thick snowflakes in a spring blizzard. Eventually, the outlines of the old ways became blurred. I was on the last car of a train, with the old ways disappearing into the distance. The GI Bill provided a good deal of the momentum for bringing about this change. It carried me into graduate school and eventually a PhD as a research psychologist. My family now included a son, Craig. His middle name is Stewart.

In terms of impact on my life, Robinson Lake was more like a prospector's can of starter yeast than any kind of road map. I never lost the sense that I had a special mission to make the world a better place. I never did feel that some men, by birth or heritage, were meant to be my superiors. The family life colored the people that I elected to be close to.

It was no accident that many of the scientists I worked with were also river runners, fly fishermen, and mountain climbers. Some of us skied the powder in the trees together. We learned that putting up wood for the ski cabin required about a half dozen PhDs working over a very long weekend. As a group, we learned to survive in the whitewater in an open canoe as well as in the jungle of funding agencies. My life became a partnership between science and the wilderness.

My wife, Marion, and a circle of friends and family emerged that kept me in touch with the early path to wilderness. They became companions exploring the Churchill River basin, Hudson's Bay, the Brooks Range in Alaska, and the tundra of the NW Territories. Now, at age eighty, I can see that in spite of these changes, the sense of family and Robinson Lake was never far away. Even as an adult month-long trips into the wilderness were always experienced with the appreciative eyes of an adolescent from Robinson Lake. What I could see remained new and fresh. I never got over the sense of special privilege at having been trained for wilderness by the family. In a very real sense, for me, the wilderness was home. I admit to a twinge of pity for those raised in any place other than Robinson Lake.

The science work in which I was passionately invested did not replace wilderness; rather, it seemed the two were tailored to co-exist. It will come as no surprise to the reader to hear that the basic tenet for the Institute I formed emphasizes cooperative group process rather than zero-sum games. The research group co-operates in activities that are as basic to survival in science as were putting in fall trout, making ice, or chopping wood.

Of course, some of the buildings that defined Robinson Lake are no longer there. All the original adults are gone. Buster is buried next to Grandma, Hank, and Gladys on a grassy knoll behind Grandmother's old store. Yet for me, standing at the lakeshore where our cabin used to be, I can still feel a powerful sense of place. There is an aura that speaks to the loving and caring that took place here, and I can still hear Grandma's voice saying, "Ya, Yeddy, iss gute."

CPSIA information can be obtained at www.ICGtesting.com
Printed in the USA
268403BV00004B/3/P